CAMPY VAMPY TRAMPY

MOVIE QUOTES

Compiled & Edited
by Steve Stewart

COMPANION PRESS
LAGUNA HILLS, CALIFORNIA

Companion Press
PO Box 2575, Laguna Hills, California 92654

Printed in the United States of America
First Printing 1996

Library of Congress Catalog Card Number: 95-70983

ISBN: 0-9625277-6-9

CONTENTS

ACKNOWLEDGMENTS

More than anyone else, I would like to thank my friend Gillian Flynn for her many campy, not to mention vampy and trampy, contributions to this book.

I would also like to thank Jeff Clark, Danny L. Curtis, Steve Desjardins, Reece Goddard, Merwyn Grote, Troy Hatlevig, Don Lort, Georgene Rada and Bette Siegel, for alerting me to many of the movies quoted in this book.

In addition, I wish to thank my partner, Jim Fredrickson, for his support and helpful suggestions, Boze Hadleigh for providing the inspiration for the title and Jim Fox and Gwyn Feldman for their assistance.

Last, but certainly not least, I would like to acknowledge the screenwriters. This book is dedicated to them, especially my two personal favorites, Woody Allen and Neil Simon, for without them this book would be considerably shorter and far less entertaining.

INTRODUCTION

"You don't have anything against
oral sex, do you?"
"No, I like to talk about sex as much
as the next fellow."
Stephen Nathan and Bruce Kimmel
The First Nudie Musical

Have you ever noticed how the campiest (most flamboyant, decadent and titillating) movie quotes are almost always about sex?

It's no surprise—at least to me—that the relationship between sex and camp on screen has lasted so long in a town notorious for its breakups. After all, it's only natural to laugh at what makes us nervous, and sex has always made American moviegoers *very* nervous.

And I'm just talking about "normal" sex. Mention taboos like incest, homosexuality or bestiality, and you've got the perfect recipe for sexually-repressed panic and delicious camp in all its fabulous and scandalous theatricality.

Today, in the mid-1990s, few would argue that we've heard it all on screen. The dishy double entendre and innuendo of yesterday has been edged out by a more raunchy and risqué repartee, but it is no less entertaining or memorable.

As always, these naughty barbs and attitude-laden lampoons are still associated with low-brow, low-budget indy pics and B-features. Ironically, nearly all of Hollywood's best and brightest writers have made their classic contributions to the art.

Writers like Dorothy Parker, Raymond Chandler, Billy Wilder, Mae West, Ruth Gordon, Garson Kanin, Gore Vidal, Blake Edwards, Neil Simon, Woody Allen, Mel Brooks, Buck Henry, John Hughes, Neal Israel, Pat Proft, Hugh Wilson, Joe Eszterhas, Keenen Ivory Wayans and Damon Wayans, Julie Brown, Lowell Ganz, Babaloo Mandel, Terrence McNally and Steve Martin, to name a few, have all made their marks with a pithy pun and a poison pen. Still, the genre receives little respect.

Because of its popularity, though, camp has come out of the comedy closet in recent years and crept into every other genre. So popular is camp that catty put-downs and trashy retorts—once uttered exclusively by dumb blondes and effeminate male extras—have now become the trademark of pumped-up action stars like Arnold Schwarzenegger, Sylvester Stallone and Steven Seagal.

As a tribute to the talented screenwriters who make us nervous and make us laugh, I've put together this collection of 901 of my favorite sassy, rude, crude and, of course, campy movie lines.

It's not that I'd ever really want this genre to achieve respectability. That, I suspect, would take away all the fun. I simply want to share a few nervous laughs with those of you who can still appreciate good oral sex—with style.

Steve Stewart
Laguna Hills, California, 1996

AGE

"You're only young once, but you can be
   immature forever."

Anthony Perkins
Mahogany (1975)

"I swear I'm aging about as well as a beach-
   party movie."

Harvey Fierstein
Torch Song Trilogy (1988)

"You're immature, Fielding."
"How am I immature?"
"Emotionally, sexually and intellectually."
"Yeah, but what other ways?"

Louise Lasser and Woody Allen
Bananas (1971)

"I think you're an asshole. Let me correct that,
   an immature asshole."

George Grizzard
Bachelor Party (1984)

"I've seen the future. It's a bald-headed man
    from New York."

Albert Brooks
Lost In America (1985)

"You must have been full of fire in your
    youth."
"I had to carry fire insurance until I was over
    forty."

Unidentified and W.C. Fields
Mississippi (1935)

"I'm at my sexual peak. Once a guy hits
    eighteen it's all down hill."
"But it's a lovely ride."

Ken Olandt and Mark Harmon
Summer School (1987)

"There's only one thing in the world worth
    having and that is youth."

George Sanders
The Picture Of Dorian Gray (1945)

"Eighteen. Is there any word in the English
    language as sexy as that?"

Robin Williams
The World According To Garp (1982)

"My dear, when you are as old as I am, you
    take your men as you find them—that is,
    if you can find them."

Helen Broderick
Top Hat (1935)

"Want to take it out in trade?"
"What do you have that's worth that much?"
"Like antiques?"

Walter Matthau and Glenda Jackson
Hopscotch (1980)

"What do I want to be when I grow up?
    Young."

Vicki Frederick
A Chorus Line (1985)

"I've aged, Sidney. I'm getting lines in my face.
    I look like a brand-new steel-belted-radial
    tire."

Maggie Smith
California Suite (1989)

"Do you mind if I sit down, I've been on my
    feet for the last fifty-six years."

Shirley MacLaine
Used People (1992)

"If I'd get back my youth, I'd do anything in
    the world—except get up early, take
    exercise or be respectable."
                                George Sanders
                    The Picture Of Dorian Gray (1945)

"Who wants to live to be ninety-five?"
"Ninety-four-year-olds."
                    William Petersen and unidentified
                                Passed Away (1992)

"It's a real pleasure to meet you, sir."
"You can drop the 'sir' if you like. I missed the
    Civil War by a good five years."
                            Rip Torn and Bob Hope
                            Critic's Choice (1963)

"It's good to see you've reached a new level of
    maturity."
"Oh, bite me."
                    Victor Garber and Michael J. Fox
                            Life With Mikey (1994)

"Time does flit, oh shit!"
                            Jennifer Jason Leigh
            Mrs. Parker And The Vicious Circle (1994)

"Did you have fun?"
"Honey, fun is like insurance—the older you
    get the more it costs."
Gladys George and David Brian
Flamingo Road (1949)

"Do you find me desirable?"
"Oh, no, Mrs. Robinson. I think you're the most
    attractive of all my parents' friends."
Anne Bancroft and Dustin Hoffman
The Graduate (1967)

"Do you know what I think when I see a pretty
    girl? Oh, to be eighty again!"
Louis Calhern
The Magnificent Yankee (1951)

"If peeing your pants is cool, consider me Miles
    Davis."
Unidentified
Billy Madison (1995)

"I can feel the blood pounding through your
    varicose veins."
Jimmy Durante
The Man Who Came To Dinner (1941)

"When a girl's under twenty-one she's
   protected by the law; when she's over sixty-
   five, she's protected by nature; anywhere in
   between, she's fair game."

Cary Grant
Operation Petticoat (1959)

"As Freud said, when you reach a certain age,
   sex becomes incongruous."

Gloria Talbot
All That Heaven Allows (1955)

"If you weren't a hundred years old I'd kick
   your wrinkled butt."

C. Thomas Howell
Nickel & Dime (1992)

"I only hope I look as good as you do when I'm
   your age."
"You did."

Ellen Burstyn and Diane Ladd
The Cemetery Club (1993)

ALCOHOL

"You know what red Ripple is don't you? Fruit punch, with a hard-on."

John Hurt
Even Cowgirls Get The Blues (1993)

"Six dollars and ninety-five cents! Would it be possible to just rent a couple of drinks?"

Jane Fonda
California Suite (1989)

"If there's one thing I have a weakness for it's champagne."
"If there's one thing I have a weakness for, it's girls who have a weakness."

Marilyn Monroe and Jack Paar
Love Nest (1951)

"He was to the bottle what Louis Armstrong was to the trumpet."

Saeed Jaffrey
My Beautiful Laundrette (1986)

"He could use a gift certificate to the Betty Ford
     Clinic."

John Turturro
Brain Donors (1992)

"I'd like to throw up but the room's too small."
Richard Pryor
California Suite (1989)

"Two [drinks], and I'm anybody's."
"Three, and I'm everybody's."
"Four, and I'm nobody's"
John Polson, Russell Crowe and Jack Thompson
The Sum Of Us (1995)

"What a nasty streak you have when you
     drink. Also when you eat and sit and walk."
Michael Caine
California Suite (1989)

"Are you out of vitamins?"
"I took a bottle yesterday, Ma. A whole fifth."
Marion Lorne and Robert Walker
Strangers On A Train (1951)

"Jim Beam me up."

George Takei
Oblivion (1995)

"How about a little gin rummy?"
"I don't drink. Never touch it."
William Demarest and Torben Meyer
Sullivan's Travels (1941)

"Even though a number of people have tried,
no one has yet found a way to drink for a
living."

Unidentified
That Certain Feeling (1956)

"What the hell is this place? Must be one of
those gay, Arab, biker sushi bars."

Unidentified
Protocol (1984)

"This is the way I look when I'm sober. It's
enough to make a person want to drink."
Lee Remick
The Days Of Wine And Roses (1962)

"One more drink and I'll be under the host."
Jennifer Jason Leigh
Mrs. Parker And The Vicious Circle (1994)

"Swan Lake always makes me terribly thirsty."
"It must have something to do with those long
    necks."
Myrna Loy and Herbert Marshall
Midnight Lace (1960)

"You're being arrested for drunk driving."
"Drunk definitely. I don't know if you could
    call it driving."
Judd Nelson and Rob Lowe
St. Elmo's Fire (1985)

"If I had to worry about getting home every-
    time I've had four or five stinger,s I'd give
    up driving."
Barbara Harris
Plaza Suite (1971)

"You don't want to become the town drunk,
    Eddie—not in Manhattan!"
Jennifer Jason Leigh
Mrs. Parker And The Vicious Circle (1994)

"One's too many and a hundred's not enough."
Unidentified
The Lost Weekend (1945)

"What are you trying to do, drown your
   troubles?"
"No, I'm just teaching them to swim."
Unidentified and Bob Hope
Critic's Choice (1963)

"Are you airsick?"
"No, someone put too many olives in my
   martini last night."
Unidentified and W.C. Fields
Never Give A Sucker An Even Break (1941)

"I'll have an Episcopalian."
"What's an Episcopalian?"
"It's like a Presbyterian except with ginger ale."
Ted Danson and J.C. Quinn
Pontiac Moon (1995)

"What's your pleasure?"
"What you got looks good."
"I know, but I thought you'd like a drink first."
Peter Falk and unidentified
The Cheap Detective (1978)

"Where would the living room be?"
"In there, but they keep the liquor locked up."
"That's alright, I always carry my own keys."

Fred MacMurray and unidentified
Double Indemnity (1944)

"Sometimes it amazes me that you ever passed
   the bar."
"I'm sure it does—you've never passed a bar in
   your life."

Shelley Long and Tom Hanks
The Money Pit (1986)

"Mac, you ever been in love?"
"No, I've been a bartender all my life."

Henry Fonda and Farrell MacDonald
My Darling Clementine (1946)

"You're invited to my cocktail party tomorrow
   night at ten o'clock. You drink don't you?"
"Yes, of course."
"Good, bring liquor."

Charles Boyer and Jane Fonda
Barefoot In The Park (1967)

"Could you be persuaded to have a drink,
    dear?"
"Well, maybe just a tiny triple."

Lucille Ball and Beatrice Arthur
Mame (1974)

"I've got a Ph.D. in cultural anthropology but I
    just love bartending."

David Foley
It's Pat—The Movie (1995)

"Who do you have to fuck to get a drink
    around here?"

Cliff Gorman
The Boys In The Band (1970)

"Who do you have to fuck to get a drink
    around here?"

Miguel Ferrer
The Harvest (1992)

"Do you want a beer?"
"It's seven o'clock in the morning!"
"Scotch?"

Michael Keaton and Martin Mull
Mr. Mom (1983)

THREE

ATHLETES

"If you can't be an athlete, be an athletic
   supporter."

Eve Arden
Grease (1978)

"I'm making an exception tonight. I usually
   don't bring home drunk, lonely young
   studs."

Andrea Naschak
Hold Me, Thrill Me, Kiss Me (1992)

"Nature built Nijinski to dance—me to direct
   traffic."

Uma Thurman
Even Cowgirls Get The Blues (1993)

"They say for every hour you exercise you add
   an hour to your life, but who needs all that
   extra time if you're going to spend it
   exercising?"

Bruce Willis
North (1994)

"He carries the Charles Atlas seal of approval."
Tim Curry
The Rocky Horror Picture Show (1975)

"This farcical show of force was only to be
    expected—the great powers flexing their
    muscles like so many impotent beach boys."
Charles Gray
Diamonds Are Forever (1971)

"I'd never sleep with a player hittin' under two
    hundred unless he had a lot of RBIs and
    was a great glove man up the middle."
Susan Sarandon
Bull Durham (1988)

"I was the intellectual equivalent of a ninety-
    eight-pound weakling. I would go to the
    beach and people would kick copies of
    Byron in my face."
Robin Williams
Dead Poets Society (1989)

"There are only two things I do really well
    sweetheart, and skating's the other one."
D.B. Sweeney
The Cutting Edge (1992)

"I beg of you, don't waste your life in the
    endless pursuit of pleasure, just running
    from woman to woman."
"Don't worry about my running, I'm in terrific
    condition."

Debbie Reynolds and Walter Matthau
Goodbye Charlie (1964)

"Boy, I couldn't save a clam from a bowl of
    chowder."

Bob Hope
Paleface (1948)

"What do you think I am—your trampoline?"

Saeed Jaffrey
My Beautiful Laundrette (1986)

"Honey, baseball's not my game."

Antonio Fargas
Car Wash (1976)

"What do you do with an elephant with three
    balls? You walk him and pitch to the rhino."

Unidentified
Hot Shots! (1991)

"You need an intelligent, sensitive man who
     can skate."

Mark Harmon
Summer School (1987)

"Could you sweat the other way, please."

Tom Hanks
The Money Pit (1986)

What you need is a good bodyguard."
"What I need is a good body! The one I've got
     isn't worth guarding."

Chico Marx and Groucho Marx
A Night In Casablanca (1946)

"I can be butch when I have to—I get it from
     my mother."

Peter Friedman
Single White Female (1992)

FOUR

BAD LUCK

"I see a clown in your future."

Tom Kenny
Shakes The Clown (1992)

"You hate people!"
"But I love gatherings. Isn't it ironic?"

Brian O'Halloran and Jeff Anderson
Clerks (1995)

"The world's an asshole and we're its farts."

Lotte Huber
Anita: Dances Of Vice (1987)

"I always get the fuzzy end of the lollipop."

Marilyn Monroe
Some Like It Hot (1959)

"I know we have a gentleman's agreement, but unfortunately I am no gentleman."

Miriam Hopkins
Design For Living (1933)

"Are you out of your mind? We're up the creek
    and you want to hock the paddle."

Jack Lemmon
Some Like It Hot (1959)

"My mother died when I was six. My father
    raped me when I was twelve."
"So you had six relatively good years."

Unidentified and Dudley Moore
Arthur (1981)

"You know, it takes two to get one in trouble."

Mae West
She Done Him Wrong (1933)

"All my life I've been waiting for someone, and
    when I find her, she's a fish."
"Nobody said love is perfect."

Tom Hanks and John Candy
Splash (1984)

"Like a midget at a urinal, I was going to have
    to stay on my toes."

Leslie Nielsen
Naked Gun 33-1/3: The Final Insult (1993)

"Guests, like fish, begin to stink on the third
    day."
"Yeah, that sounds about right. Actually, I think
    you'll find I begin to stink on the first day."
Taylor Nichols and Chris Eigeman
Barcelona (1994)

"I can't believe I gave my panties to a geek."
Molly Ringwald
Sixteen Candles (1984)

"How could you sleep with me?"
"You slept with me."
"Yeah, but that's because I thought you were
    someone else."
Annabella Sciorra and Kevin Anderson
The Night We Never Met (1993)

"You've got the mind of a pig."
"It's a pig's world."
Katharine Hepburn and Cary Grant
Sylvia Scarlett (1935)

FIVE

BEAUTY

"When you've got a hump back, why spend money on a nose job?"

Shirley MacLaine
Used People (1992)

"Give me cheek bones or give me death!"

Meshach Taylor
Mannequin Two: On The Move (1991)

"Beauty is only skin deep."
"That's deep enough for me."

Bud Abbott and Lou Costello
Rio Rita (1942)

"Underneath that pose is just more pose."

Lenny Baker
Next Stop, Greenwich Village (1976)

"He has unnatural, natural beauty."

Leonard Frey
The Boys In The Band (1970)

"When the going gets tough, the tough get
    gorgeous!"

Craig Russell
Too Outrageous! (1987)

"Physical beauty isn't everything."
"Thank you, Quasimodo."

Leonard Frey and Kenneth Nelson
The Boys In The Band (1970)

"I figured, as long as I had to suffer I might as
    well get a tan."

Harry Hamlin
Making Love (1982)

"He's not just a pretty face, he's also a great
    body."

Moira Kelly
With Honors (1994)

"I saw your show the other night on
    radioactive isotopes and I just have one
    question—is that your real hair?"

Joanne Baron
Real Genius (1985)

"It's better to be looked over than overlooked."
Mae West
Belle Of The Nineties (1934)

"Don't ever change."
"I try not to, but the bills at the beauty parlor
    get bigger every year."
Doris Day and Myrna Loy
Midnight Lace (1960)

"I know I may look like a rhinoceros, but I
    have quite a thin skin, really."
Minnie Driver
Circle Of Friends (1994)

"If you marry a pretty girl she's liable to run
    away."
"Isn't a homely girl liable to run away too?"
"Yeah, but who cares?"
Unidentified
Buck Privates Come Home (1947)

"The ugly may be beautiful, but the pretty,
    never."
Unidentified
Even Cowgirls Get The Blues (1993)

"I think that's good business—to surround
    yourself with ugly women and beautiful
    men."

Rita Hayworth
Gilda (1946)

"I suppose if Ginny stays she'll grow up to look
    like that: blonde hair, blonde teeth, blonde
    life."

Jane Fonda
California Suite (1989)

"I'm not knocking Urno. He's great, if you
    happen to like a tall, blond, crushing,
    Nordic, Aryan, Nazi type."

Woody Allen
Sleeper (1973)

"I think you're just jealous that I'm a genuine
    freak and you have to wear a mask."

Danny De Vito
Batman Returns (1992)

"Bad makeup is not unique to the West."

John Lone
M Butterfly (1993)

"Sidney, was I hit by a bus? I look as though I
　　were hit by a fully-loaded, guided-tour bus."
　　　　　　　　　　　　　　　　Maggie Smith
　　　　　　　　　　　　California Suite (1989)

"I just got your call. I was having a manicure."
"At two o'clock in the morning?"
"I cannot sleep with long fingernails."
　　　　　　　　　　Peter Lorre and Jules Munshin
　　　　　　　　　　　　　Silk Stockings (1957)

"I must have your golden hair, fascinating eyes,
　　alluring smile, your lovely arms, your form
　　divine."
"Wait a minute. Is this a proposal or are you
　　taking inventory?"
　　　　　　　　　　　John Miljan and Mae West
　　　　　　　　　Belle Of The Nineties (1934)

"What the hell happened to you?"
"I was attacked by a roving band of drunken
　　cosmetologists, can't you tell?"
"I think you might be entitled to a refund."
　　　　　　Jonathan Silverman and Adrienne Shelly
　　　　　　　　　　　Teresa's Tattoo (1994)

"Don't tell my dad about this, he'll have my
    head."
"Then where would you put your hair!"
    Jeffrey Tambor and Mary Stuart Masterson
    Radioland Murders (1994)

"What is he, a psychiatrist or a hairdresser?"
"Actually he's both. He shrinks my head and
    them combs me out."
    Kenneth Nelson and Frederick Combs
    The Boys In The Band (1970)

"You are so much less attractive when I'm
    sober."
"Thank goodness it's not that often."
    Shelley Long and Tom Hanks
    The Money Pit (1986)

"I don't know if anyone's ever mentioned this
    to you before, but it looks to me like you
    could be shaving in the wrong direction."
    Jack Gilpin
    Barcelona (1994)

"The glamour has left the building."
    Lori Petty
    Tank Girl (1995)

"I'll have my double chins in private."

Marie Dressler
Dinner At Eight (1933)

"I feel ridiculous. I think you put too much
　　makeup on me."
"There's no such thing as too much makeup."

Ellen Burstyn and Diane Lada
The Cemetery Club (1993)

"I've told you a million times not to talk to me
　　when I'm doing my lashes."

Jean Harlow
Dinner At Eight (1933)

"People who are very beautiful make their own
　　laws."

Vivien Leigh
The Roman Spring Of Mrs. Stone (1961)

"You're the most beautiful woman I've ever
　　seen, which doesn't say much for you."

Groucho Marx
Animal Crackers (1930)

"He runs four miles a day and has a body like
   Mark Spitz. Unfortunately, he still has a face
   like Ernest Borgnine."

Ellen Burstyn
Same Time, Next Year (1978)

"If a caterpillar was afraid of wings, it would
   never become a butterfly, and people would
   say, 'Hey look. It's a worm in a tree.'"

Hollis McLaren,
Outrageous! (1977)

"There are some beautiful women in Tunis."
"I'm not interested in beautiful women."
"Well, in that case, you should look up some of
   the women I've taken out."

Groucho Marx and Sig Ruman
A Night In Casablanca

"I've gone out with some bums in my day, but
   they were beautiful. That is the only reason
   to go out with a bum."

Mercedes Ruehl
The Fisher King (1991)

"If she were a President, she'd be Babe-raham
    Lincoln."

Dana Carvey
Wayne's World (1992)

"I just jove your hair, it's so soft and silky."
"Silky now, but next year I'm getting nylon."
Lisette Verea and Groucho Marx
A Night In Casablanca

"You are sort of attractive, in a corn-fed sort of
    way. I can imagine some poor girl falling for
    you if—well, if you threw in a set of
    dishes."

Bette Davis
The Man Who Came To Dinner (1941)

"You're looking good. Who's your embalmer?"
Juliette Lewis
The Basketball Diaries (1995)

"Nice hairdo, you get FM on that?"
Keanu Reeves
The Night Before (1988)

SIX

BISEXUALITY

"If there's anything I hate, it's a bisexual
    homosexual—or is it the other way
    around?"
"It works either way."
                    Maggie Smith and Michael Caine
                    California Suite (1989)

"You know, this wife swapping business wasn't
    such a bad idea."
"I only hope our wives are hitting it off this
    well."
                                    Unidentified
        If You Don't Stop It…You'll Go Blind (1978)

"It was like electricity."
"I know, that wonderful AC/DC feeling, but
    that's not love."
"Oh, it's close enough."
                    Jayne Mansfield and Joan Blondell
                    Will Success Spoil Rock Hunter? (1957)

"You prefer nymphs to satyrs?"
"I like both, lord."

Malcolm McDowell and unidentified
Caligula (1979)

"Gee you're pretty."
"I bet you say that to all the girls."
"Yes, it don't go over so good with the boys."

Lou Costello and unidentified
Abbott And Costello Meet The Killer (1949)

"I played the bride, now I get to play the
    groom."

Perry King
A Different Story (1979)

"I'd like you to meet a friend of mine. He
    specializes in sexual ambivalence."

Joseph Scorsiani
Naked Lunch (1991)

CHEATING

"I can't believe this, both of my boyfriends are
  cheating on me!"

Heather Graham
Don't Do It! (1995)

"I'm so disappointed in you. It's so damned
  unoriginal. Everyone cheats with their
  secretary, I expected more from my
  husband."

Maureen Stapleton
Plaza Suite (1971)

"Why are you always so shy?"
"Why are you always so married?"

Unidentified and Dudley Moore
Like Father Like Son (1987)

"I've been married six months and haven't had
  an affair."
"It can happen."

Julie Christie and George C. Scott
Petulia (1968)

"Oh my God, I slept with the wrong guy!
    The one time in my life I cheat and I screw
    it up."

Annabella Sciorre
The Night We Never Met (1993)

"My imagination? I saw you two locked
    together in her dressing room like Siamese
    twins attached at the zipper!"

Mary Stuart Masterson
Radioland Murders (1994)

"What are we going to do?"
"You're taken care of, you're having an affair.
    I'm the one who needs an activity."

Walter Matthau and Maureen Stapleton
Plaza Suite (1971)

"I've respected your husband for many years,
    and what's good enough for him is good
    enough for me."

Groucho Marx
Monkey Business (1931)

"Someone once said fidelity is a fading
   woman's protection and a charming
   woman's weakness."

Douglas Fairbanks, Jr.
The Prisoner Of Zenda (1937)

"I don't like no one fooling around with my
   gal."
"I got news for you, I ain't fooling."

Jeff York and Bob Hope
Paleface (1948)

"Beg your pardon ... what the girl does here is
   our affair. Your affair is to get her back so
   that she can continue doing it."

Wilfred Hyde-White
My Fair Lady (1964)

"I'm sick of the hot clubs, the hot cars, the hot
   chicks. I'm sick of all the fun—I want you."

Andrew Dice Clay
The Adventures Of Ford Fairlane (1990)

"I've never cheated before, you know."
"Cheated? Cheating is when it's for fun. This
    is business, like a doctor seeing a patient."
Barbra Streisand and Molly Picon
For Pete's Sake (1974)

"Why is it the only time a wife knows how you
    feel is when you feel it for another woman?"
Unidentified
How To Save A Marriage (And Ruin Your Life)
(1968)

"I wasn't made to be a housewife."
"Some of my best friends are housewives."
Thelma Todd and Groucho Marx
Monkey Business (1931)

"I really mean it this time."
"Mean what?"
"Marriage and all that."
"No, I'm afraid it would be too little marriage
    and too much all that."
Unidentified and Gloria Swanson
Indiscreet (1931)

"When you're in love with a married man you
  shouldn't wear mascara."
Shirley MacLaine
The Apartment (1960)

"I've trusted men all my life and I've never
  been deceived yet—except by my
  husbands—and they don't count."
Mary Boland
He Married His Wife (1940)

"I'm afraid after we've been married awhile a
  beautiful young girl will come along and
  you'll forget all about me."
"Don't be silly, I'll write you twice a week."
Margaret Dumont and Groucho Marx
The Big Store (1941)

"Do you talk to your wife while having sex?"
"Yes, if I happen to be near the phone."
Unidentified
If You Don't Stop It…You'll Go Blind (1978)

EIGHT

CHILDREN

"You have the sophistication of a woman of
    twelve."

Blake McIver Ewing
The Little Rascals (1994)

"If you were my kids I'd punish you."
"If we were your kids we'd punish ourselves."
Mel Brooks and Kevin Jamal Woods
The Little Rascals (1994)

"You had sex with your sister?"
"She was five, I was four—it was consentual."
Unidentified and Todd Field
Sleep With Me (1994)

"Have you ever had a talk with him about, you
    know, girls?"
"Yeah, a few times, but he wouldn't give me
    any phone numbers."
Ethel Merman and Dan Daly
There's No Business Like Show Business (1945)

"You can't treat people this way, mister."
"You're not people, you're kids."
> *Travis Tedford and Mel Brooks*
> *The Little Rascals* (1994)

"Your full name's Bill?"
"My parents didn't believe in padding."
> *Alexis Arquette and Bill Rotko*
> *Grief* (1994)

"You're the best son money can buy."
> *Donald Trump*
> *The Little Rascals* (1994)

"I can cook a little. I can take care of the
children. If there are no children, I can take
care of that."
> *Eddie Cantor*
> *Roman Scandals* (1933)

"We're getting married soon, let's take a
chance—play some Russian roulette."
"And guess who has to carry the bullet around
for nine months."
> *Judd Nelson and Ally Sheedy*
> *St. Elmo's Fire* (1985)

"Nothing offends me. When I was eleven I
    walked in on my father and the Shetland
    pony he gave me for my tenth birthday.
    Does that excite you?"
"I don't know, I never met your father."
                    Priscilla Presley and Andrew Dice Clay
                    The Adventures Of Ford Fairlane (1990)

"Doctor, I have a girl of nine that never listens
    to what's right. She's always doing the
    wrong thing. What should I do?"
"Well, wait another ten years, and if there's no
    improvement, mail me her phone number."
                    Unidentified and Bob Hope
                    My Favorite Blonde (1942)

"Can't you see I love you and want you for the
    father of my children?"
"I didn't know you had any."
                    Virginia O'Brien and Red Skelton
                    DuBarry Was A Lady (1943)

"What's the difference between a light bulb and
    a pregnant woman? You can unscrew a
    light bulb."

                    Steve Martin
                    My Blue Heaven (1990)

"You know why Santa Claus can't father a
    child? Because he comes down the
    chimney."

Unidentified
The World According To Garp (1982)

"It's a very awkward age for girls."
"What age is that?"
"Twelve through thirty-five."

Paul Reiser and Matthew Modine
Bye Bye Love (1995)

"What the hell you doing kid?"
"I had to go to the bathroom."
"On my head?"
"Hey, buddy, this is my bathroom, not your
    bedroom."

Bobcat Goldthwait and Paige Cosney
Shakes The Clown (1992)

"What do you say we slip into the backseat and
    you make a man out of me?"
"What do you say I slap you around for
    awhile?"
"Can't we do both?"

Unidentified and Geena Davis
A League Of Their Own (1992)

"Do you often see your father?"
"No, we're just good friends."
Unidentified and Paul McCartney
A Hard Day's Night (1964)

"I took the liberty of bringing my little boy for
    an examination. He's developed a very
    peculiar and unpleasant habit."
"Ah yes, breathing, no doubt."
Unidentified and Bob Hope
My Favorite Blonde (1942)

"What's this obsession you have with girls?"
"I was a poor kid, remember. I didn't have toys
    to play with."
Tony Randall and Rock Hudson
Lover Come Back (1961)

"Have you ever been with a man?"
"Well, just with my brother."
Veronica Forque and Rossy de Palma
Kika (1993)

"Did your mother have any kids that lived?"
Corey Feldman
Stand By Me (1986)

CLOTHING

"Oh, I have the napkins that match your hat."
Goldie Hawn
Protocol (1984)

"If that dress had pockets, you'd look like a
pool table."
Rodney Dangerfield
Back To School (1986)

"Remember, my people, there is no shame in
being poor ... only [in] dressing poorly."
George Hamilton
Zorro, The Gay Blade (1981)

"If I don't come up with a cheaper solution, I'm
going to end up a bag lady. Of course, I'll
have alligator bags."
Demi Moore
St. Elmo's Fire (1985)

"It's a lovely gown. It's a shame they didn't
    have it in your size. "

                                        Unidentified
                            Vegas In Space (1993)

"Anyone can rob a bank, but it takes a real man
    to do it in satin."

                                        Jon Polito
                              Blankman (1994)

If I'd known my blotches would turn purple,
    I'd have bought bags to match."

                                   Stephen Spinella
                      And The Band Played On (1994)

"Can I interest you in a nightcap?"
"No thanks, I don't wear them."

                        Priscilla Presley and Leslie Nielsen
                              The Naked Gun (1988)

"We can't talk to them, they're practically
    naked."
"Imagine them with clothes on."

                        Michael Caine and Joseph Bologna
                              Blame It On Rio (1984)

'Now remember, it's BYOL—bring your own
  leather."

Jean Smart
Protocol (1984)

'I rather like my apartment. It's just big enough
  to lay my hat and a few friends."

Jennifer Jason Leigh
Mrs. Parker And The Vicious Circle (1994)

'Well, I always say, you never really get to
  know a person until they put their clothes
  on."

Carol Burnett
Who's Been Sleeping In My Bed? (1963)

"Maybe you shouldn't dress like that."
"This is a blouse and a skirt. I don't know what
  you're talking about."
"Maybe you shouldn't wear that body."

William Hurt and Kathleen Turner
Body Heat (1991)

"Oh my God! Someone's been sleeping in my
  dress."

Beatrice Arthur
Mame (1974)

"I know exactly how you feel, my dear. The
    morning after always looks grim if you
    happen to be wearing last night's dress."
                                        Ina Claire
                                    Ninotchka (1939)

"The thing that separates us from the animals is
    our ability to accessorize."
                                    Olympia Dukakis
                                Steel Magnolias (1989)

"This is very unusual. I've never been alone
    with a man before—even with my dress
    on."
                        Audrey Hepburn and Gregory Peck
                                Roman Holiday (1953)

"I can never get a zipper to close. Maybe that
    stands for something. What do you think?"
                                    Rita Hayworth
                                    Gilda (1946)

"You think anybody with pants is cute."
"That's a lie. I like lots of people without
    pants."
                                    Unidentified
                                Pal Joey (1957)

CROSS-DRESSING

"Why don't you take your dress off and fight like a man."

Michael Greer
The Gay Deceivers (1969)

"I'm telling you, if I didn't have a dress on, I'd kick his arrogant ass in."

Dustin Hoffman
Tootsie (1982)

"It's gorgeous. Let's face it Roger, that dress is you."

Zero Mostel
The Producers (1968)

"Now I know why drag queens drink from such big glasses! To make their hands look smaller!"

Sarah Chadwick
The Adventures Of Priscilla, Queen Of The Desert
(1994)

"Hot dog, you got a great set of knockers there
   Steve."

Ramona Fischer
Vegas In Space (1993)

"What's more boring than a queen doing a
   Judy Garland imitation?"
"A queen doing a Bette Davis imitation."

Kenneth Nelson and Frederick Combs
The Boys In The Band (1970)

"It works, but don't play hard to get."

Sydney Pollack
Tootsie (1982)

"If we ever get out of this, things are going to
   be different, I promise you. I'm going to be
   the man I was when we first met."
"You weren't blonde then, and you wore a lot
   less makeup."

John Ritter and Pam Dawber
Stay Tuned (1992)

"Henri, remember, you're a lady."

Ann Sheridan
I Was A Male War Bride (1940)

"The wedding was gorgeous. The best man
      gave the groom away, my father gave the
      bride away, and the fact that I wanted to be
      flower girl gave me away."

Michael Greer
The Gay Deceivers (1969)

"Ninety-percent of all women today are men."

Eric Schaeffer
My Life's In Turnaround (1994)

"I'll reason with him."
"Oh, sure, you're going to reason with a grown
      man in a dress?"

Malcolm Dundas and Kevin Dillon
Heaven Help Us (1985)

"I was a better man with you, as a woman, than
      I ever was with a woman, as a man. Know
      what I mean? I just gotta learn to do it
      without the dress."

Dustin Hoffman
Tootsie (1982)

"I'm suppose to be the grand duchess
   Anastasia, but I think I look more like
   Tugboat Annie."

Christopher Hewett
The Producers (1968)

"I can waltz in like Ozzie or I can waltz in like
   Harriet, but I can't waltz in like Ozzie and
   Harriet. It's just too taxing."

Wallace Shawn
Scenes From The Class Struggle In Beverly Hills
(1989)

"Are you unhappy because you didn't get to
   wear my dress?"
"If I had worn your dress it would have hung
   properly."

Maggie Smith and Michael Caine
California Suite (1989)

"There's nothing more inconvenient than an
   old queen with a head cold."

Robert Preston
Victor/Victoria (1983)

"I feel like Gloria Swanson."
"You look like her mother."
Robin Williams and Harvey Fierstein
Mrs. Doubtfire (1993)

"I don't want to go on, night after night,
   painting my face."
Albert Finney
The Dresser (1983)

"Since when has it been a crime to play
   charades?"
Glenda Jackson
Salome's Last Dance (1987)

"It's a busy life. Places to go, faces to paint."
Harvey Fierstein
Mrs. Doubtfire (1993)

"You almost look like a man today Edna."
"So do you Alex."
Tom McGowan and Lili Taylor
Mrs. Parker And The Vicious Circle (1994)

ELEVEN

DATING

"[In] time you'll meet someone very special.
   Someone who won't press charges."

Raul Julia
Addams Family Values (1993)

"I know this is our first date but do you think
   the next time you make love to your
   boyfriend you could think of me?"

Steve Martin
The Jerk (1979)

"No more dates."
"Don't think of him as a date, think of him as a
   meal."

Lucille Ball and Van Johnson
Yours, Mine And Ours (1968)

"I wasn't dating him, I was fucking him."

Sharon Stone
Basic Instinct (1992)

"You're a regular James Bond, man."
"Yeah, except James Bond had Pussy Galore
and I can't even get a date."
Nick Corri and Anthony Edwards
Gotcha! (1985)

"I'm not interested in beautiful women."
"Then you ought to look up some of the girls
I've taken out."
Unidentified and Groucho Marx
A Night In Casablanca (1946)

"I have two rules. One, I do not date musicians.
Two, I do not kill people."
Erika Eleniak
Under Siege (1992)

"What are you doing Saturday night?"
"Committing suicide."
"What are you doing Friday night?"
Woody Allen and Diana Davila
Play It Again, Sam (1972)

"How was jail? Meet anyone?"
Pauly Shore
Encino Man (1992)

"Some people play hard to get. I play hard to
    want."

Andrew Dice Clay
The Adventures Of Ford Fairlane (1990)

"When we were dating we spent most of our
    time talking about sex—why I couldn't do
    it, where could we do it, were her parents
    going to go out so we could do it …
    Married, we've just got nothing to talk
    about."

Daniel Stern
Diner (1982)

"A woman who wants someone like me goes to
    the pound and gets a three-legged dog."

Jon Lovitz
City Slickers II: The Legend Of Curly's Gold (1994)

"Aren't we still friends?"
"No, we are not friends. I don't take this shit
    from friends—only from lovers."

Dustin Hoffman and Teri Garr
Tootsie (1982)

"If I wanted a man in my life I wouldn't have
  bought a VCR."

Michelle Pfeiffer
Frankie & Johnny (1991)

"You dating yet?"
"I'm eleven."
"Yeah, always good to wait. I myself didn't
  start dating until I was eleven and a half."

Ted Danson and Macaulay Culkin
Getting Even With Dad (1994)

"I tried calling but they didn't have a listing for
  Mr. Wonderful."
"What spelling did you use?"

Cindy Morgan and Chevy Chase
Caddyshack (1980)

"Ed, have you noticed the older you get, the
  younger your girlfriends get? Soon, you'll
  be dating sperm."

Billy Crystal
City Slickers (1991)

TWELVE

DEATH

"If I die I'm sorry for all the bad things I did to you. And if I live I'm sorry for all the bad things I'm going to do to you."

Roy Scheider
All That Jazz (1979)

"*Romeo and Juliet* is a play about love and sex and people who were willing to die for it."
"I'm dying for it right now."

Unidentified and Matt Dillon
My Bodyguard (1980)

"This is a wake, not a garage sale!"

Bob Hoskins
Passed Away (1992)

"What did you do to your wrists?"
"I cut myself shaving."

Barry Tubb and Kelly Lynch
Warm Summer Rain (1990)

"If you really want to stare death in the eye,
you should have gotten married."

Dale Swann
Tango & Cash (1989)

"In our family we don't divorce our men—we
bury them."

Ruth Gordon
Lord Love A Duck (1966)

"When I die, in the newspapers they'll write
that the sons of bitches of this world
have lost their leader."

Vincent Gardenia
Bang The Drum Slowly (1973)

"What do you give a suicidal patient who has
everything?"
"A parachute."

Bruce Willis and Scott Bakula
The Color Of Night (1994)

"You're just walking around to save funeral
expenses."

Valerie Perrine
The Electric Horseman (1979)

"What would you do if you were me?"
"Kill myself."

> *Ernie Lively and Wesley Snipes*
> *Passenger 57* (1992)

"Razors pain you, rivers are damp. Acids stain
you and drugs cause cramp. Guns aren't
lawful, nooses give. Gas smells awful,
might as well live."

> *Jennifer Jason Leigh*
> *Mrs. Parker And The Vicious Circle* (1994)

"I know Felix, he's too nervous to kill himself.
He wears his seat belt in the drive-in
movie."

> *Walter Matthau*
> *The Odd Couple* (1968)

"Someone has killed herself for love of you. I
do wish that I had had such an experience.
The women who have admired me…have
all insisted on living on long after I have
ceased to care for them."

> *George Sanders*
> *The Picture Of Dorian Gray* (1945)

That's the most uncomfortable coffin I've ever
    been in."

> *Martin Landau*
> *Ed Wood* (1994)

Life after death is as improbable as sex after
    marriage."

> *Madeline Kahn*
> *Clue* (1985)

Do the world a favor, pull your lip over your
    head and swallow."

> *Walter Matthau*
> *Grumpy Old Men* (1994)

Thank you, that was very good."
What's the difference, in a hundred years we'll
    both be dead."
I'm not sure I can wait that long."

> *Nathan Lane and Jonathan Charles Kaplan*
> *Life With Mikey* (1994)

He came back from the dead for me."
God, my boyfriend wouldn't even pump gas
    for me."

> *Traci Lind and Unidentified*
> *My Boyfriend's Back* (1993)

"Sam, there is no reason for anything."
"Remind me never to invite you to a funeral."
Tim Guinee and Matthew Broderic
The Night We Never Met (1993

"If you want to commit suicide, use my razor.
    It's electric but you can hang yourself on the
    cord."

Gig Youn
Strange Bedfellows (1964

"If the honeymoon doesn't work out, let's not
    get divorced, let's kill each other."
"Let's have one of the maids do it. I hear the
    service here is wonderful."
Jane Fonda and Robert Redfor
Barefoot In The Park (1967

"There's a lot of prejudice against the undead."
Andrew Lower
My Boyfriend's Back (1993

"If I get killed, my blood is on your hands."
"Just don't get it on my shoes."
Harold Ramis and Bill Murra
Stripes (1981

"Today is the last day of the rest of your life."
                        Andrew Dice Clay
        The Adventures Of Ford Fairlane (1990)

"To tell you the truth, I find it quite pleasant
    being widowed."
"I look forward to it myself."
                Joan Plowright and Jeanne Moreau
                The Summer House (1994)

"I refuse to be in a club where half the
    members are dead."
                                Diane Ladd
                The Cemetery Club (1993)

"Where I grew up in Brooklyn nobody
    committed suicide, everyone was too
    unhappy."
                                Woody Allen
                Crimes And Misdemeanors (1989)

"Weddings are such a nuisance."
"I prefer funerals, the food is better."
                Joan Plowright and Maggie Steed
                The Summer House (1994)

THIRTEEN

DOCTORS

"Drop your pants."
"I don't even know your first name."
"Doctor."

Deborah Pratt and Paul Mercurio
Exit To Eden (1994)

"Have you had much experience with boys?"
"Well, once I played nurse with the boy next
   door and got sued for malpractice."
Clint Howard and Dey Young
Rock 'n' Roll High School (1979)

"All I want you to do is loosen your belt and
   say 'ah.'"

Raquel Welch
Myra Breckinridge (1970)

"The psychiatrist asked me if I thought sex was
   dirty and I said it is if you're doing it right."
Woody Allen
Take The Money And Run (1969)

"Women make the best psychoanalysts 'til they
    fall in love. After that, they make the best
    patients."

Unidentified
An American In Paris (1951)

"I went to a psychiatrist but it didn't work out.
    The psychiatrist had a couch, but it was
    built for two."

Joan Blondell
Will Success Spoil Rock Hunter? (1957)

"He's not sick, you idiot. He's dead."
"Oh, everybody's a doctor."

Paul Dooley and Austin Pendleton
My Boyfriend's Back (1993)

"What does one give to a man who has
    everything?"
"A shot of penicillin."

Emma Samms and unidentified
The Shrimp On The Barbie (1990)

FOURTEEN

ENEMIES

"Sure, forgive your enemies, but first get even."
James Cagney
Blood On The Sun (1945)

"With friends like you, who needs enemas?"
Matthew Broderick
The Road To Wellville (1994)

"I fought the war for your sort."
"I bet you're sorry you won!"
Richard Vernon and Ringo Starr
A Hard Day's Night (1964)

"Don't look at me in that tone of voice."
Jennifer Jason Leigh
Mrs. Parker And The Vicious Circle (1994)

"I wish I had a club to throw you out of."
Travis Tedford
The Little Rascals (1994)

"You shoot me in a *dream* and you better wake
    up and apologize."

Harvey Keitel
Reservoir Dogs (1992)

"You make me sick. When you can't have what
    you want, you make certain that everyone
    around is equally as miserable."
"I haven't noticed any equals around me."

Michael Caine and Maggie Smith
California Suite (1989)

"Why don't I get married again? I don't get
    married again because I can't find anyone I
    dislike enough to inflict that kind of torture
    on."

Roy Scheider
All That Jazz (1979)

"There's nothing serious between us. In fact,
    apart from music and sex we thoroughly
    dislike each other."

John Glover
A Little Sex (1982)

"It's a well-known fact that you get nauseous
    just turning around."
"That's only if you're standing behind me."
                    Shawn Phelan and Marty Belafsky
                        Breaking The Rules (1992

"Fuck 'em."
"Now you're talking my language."
                    Michael Douglas and Roma Maffi
                        Disclosure (1994

"We're not quarreling, we're in complete
    agreement. We hate each other."
                                Fred Astaire
                        The Band Wagon (1953

"I don't use a pen. I write with a goose quill
    dipped in venom."
                                Clifton Webb
                            Laura (1944

"Do you hold grudges?"
"Ask me in about ten years."
                    Paul Gunning and Donna McDaniel
                        Hollywood Hot Tubs (1984)

FIFTEEN

FANTASIES

"Is sex all you ever think about?"
"Other thoughts creep in, I just ignore them."
Lewis Alante and Slade Burrus
The Boys Of Cellblock Q (1993)

"We sell dreams. Your job is to keep the
overhead down."

Shelley Winters
The Balcony (1963)

"I've been chased by women before but not
while I was awake."

Bob Hope
Paleface (1948)

"How can I fulfill your fantasy?"
"Go paint my house."
Sean O'Bryan and Rosie O'Donnell
Exit To Eden (1994)

"It seems we've met before, perhaps in your
    dreams."
"You wouldn't be seen in those kinds of
    places."
                            Dorothy Lamour and Bob Hope
                            Road To Utopia (1945)

"Do you think it possible that someday you can
    make love with me and think of him?"
"Who knows? Maybe you and he can make
    love and you can think of me."
                        Steve Martin and Bernadette Peters
                            The Jerk (1979)

"Would you have even a vague idea what
    they're doing in there?"
"I have a very definite idea."
                            Jack Lemmon and Lou Jacobi
                            Irma La Douce (1963)

"Where have I seen you before?"
"Maybe in one of your better dreams."
                            Paul Lieber and Bridget Fonda
                            Shag —The Movie (1989)

"Don't you think it's better for a girl to be
    preoccupied with sex than occupied?"
                                        Unidentified
                                The Moon Is Blue (1953)

"I had a dream last night. It was so boring it
    woke me up."
                                        Ted Danson
                                    Body Heat (1981)

"I don't sell my fantasies."
                                        Corey Parker
                                    Biloxi Blues (1988)

"Last night never happened."
"I know, I was there when it never happened."
                        Michael Caine and Michelle Johnson
                                Blame It On Rio (1984)

SIXTEEN

FELLATIO

"You don't have anything against oral sex, do you?"
"No, I like to talk about sex as much as the next fellow."

> *Stephen Nathan and Bruce Kimmel*
> *The First Nudie Musical* (1976)

"Gertrude Stein was right. A mouth is a mouth is a mouth."

> *Ray Sharkey*
> *Scenes From The Class Struggle In Beverly Hills*
> (1989)

"My girlfriend sucked thirty-seven dicks!"
"In a row?"

> *Brian O'Halloran and unidentified*
> *Clerks* (1994)

"I'm so against working I wouldn't even take a blow job."

> *Unidentified*
> *Mo' Money* (1992)

"If you haven't gotten a blow job from a
    superior officer, well, you're just letting the
    best in life pass you by."

Jack Nicholson
A Few Good Men (1992)

"I've got a Ph.D. in oral sex."
"Did they make you take any Spanish with
    that?"

Diane Keaton and Woody Allen
Sleeper (1973)

"Who's a girl gotta suck around here to get a
    drink?"

Linda Fiorentino
The Last Seduction (1993)

"Here's to you—sucking my dick."

Andrew Dice Clay
The Adventures Of Ford Fairlane (1990)

"You took advantage of my position."
"And I might be tempted to do so again if you
    don't close your mouth."

Douglas Hodge and Nicholas Grace
Salome's Last Dance (1987)

"You know how to whistle, don't you Steve?
   You just put your lips together and blow."

Lauren Bacall
To Have And Have Not (1944)

"You stick your dick in my mouth and then you
   get an attack of morality?"

Demi Moore
Disclosure (1994)

"Suck me sideways."

Jim Carrey
Dumb & Dumber (1995)

"Which of you gorgeous guys would like to
   have your oil changed?"

Lori Petty
Tank Girl (1995)

"I wouldn't suck your lousy dick if I was
   suffocating and there was oxygen in your
   balls!"

Mink Stole
Female Trouble (1973)

F O O D

"You wanna eat some Chinese?"
"Yeah, all nine-hundred million of them."
Alan Bates and Bette Midler
The Rose (1979)

"My Swedish meatballs are dried up and my
beans are shriveled."
Perry King
A Different Story (1979)

"Anyone who can swallow two Snowballs and
a Ding Dong shouldn't have any problem
with pride."
Steve Guttenberg
Can't Stop The Music (1980)

"I think ice cream's better than sex."
"I couldn't make that comparison. I've never
had ice cream before."
Estee Chandler and Luke Perry
Terminal Bliss (1992)

"I'll sleep with you for a meatball."

Julie Andrews
Victor/Victoria (1983)

"Marriage is like a dull meal with the dessert at
   the beginning."

José Ferrer
Moulin Rouge (1952)

"I have never hidden behind closet doors, but I
   am discreet."
"Discreet! You did everything but lick his
   artichoke."

Michael Caine and Maggie Smith
California Suite (1989)

"My recipes—better burn them lest they fall
   into the wrong hands."

John Glover
An Early Frost (1985)

"Say no more darling, when Craig and I were
   first married I didn't know a thing about
   cooking either. I used to dress a turkey
   in Levis."

Michael Greer
The Gay Deceivers (1969)

"Some cultures are defined by their
  relationship to cheese."

Mary Stuart Masterson
Benny & Joon (1993)

"You got your terminology confused, we did
  not make love."
"Whatever the hell it was it beats drying the
  dishes."

George Segal and Barbra Streisand
The Owl And The Pussycat (1970)

"My life's gonna be one big happy smorgas-
  bord."
"Well, if you ever need a piece of herring, you
  know where to find me."

Dean Martin and Carol Burnette
Who's Been Sleeping In My Bed? (1963)

"I'm starved for your kisses. I'm famished for
  your love."
"You don't want me, you want the Diner's
  Club."

Anita Ekberg and Bob Hope
Paris Holiday (1958)

"Watch out—he prefers the banana to the fig."
Unidentified
Arabian Nights (1974)

"Would you like some dessert?"
"What did you have in mind?"
"How about something sweet and Southern?"
Unidentified and Chevy Chase
Fletch Lives (1989)

"Your wife is safe with Tonetti—he prefers
   spaghetti."

Erik Rhodes
The Gay Divorcee (1931)

"You have any Danish?"
"No, how about a little Greek?"
Xaviera Hollander and Unidentified
The Happy Hooker Goes To Washington (1977)

"Come on darling, you have time to buy me
   one cup of coffee."
"Not me, I haven't finished paying for the last one
   yet."

Marilyn Maxwell and Bob Hope
Critic's Choice (1963)

"Sucking the marrow out of life doesn't mean choking on the bone."

Robin Williams
Dead Poets Society (1989)

"What are we, ladies? I'll tell you what we are: waitresses at the banquet of life."

Bette Midler
The Rose (1979)

"Not too spicy, we're Jewish. We take gas very seriously."

Shirley MacLaine
Used People (1992)

"There are two things that clearly differentiate the human species from animals. One, we use cutlery; two, we control our sexual urges."

Dan Aykroyd
Dragnet (1987)

"Just because I don't know how to cook doesn't mean I don't know how to eat."

Barbra Streisand
The Prince Of Tides (1991)

"Life is a banquet and most poor suckers are
   starving to death."

> *Rosalind Russell*
> *Auntie Mame* (1958)

"I've just got to ask, what does human flesh
   taste like?"
"Chicken."

> *Emilio Estevez and unidentified*
> *National Lampoon's Loaded Weapon 1* (1993)

"I was an only child but my mother fed me as if
   I were two."

> *Minnie Driver*
> *Circle Of Friends* (1994)

"I can cook."
"You don't have to cook, I've got enough
   potato chips to last me a year."

> *Jack Lemmon and Walter Matthau*
> *The Odd Couple* (1968)

"Love is apples, marriage is oranges—not
   everybody can stomach fruit cocktail."

> *Edward Herrmann*
> *A Little Sex* (1982)

'You're a wonderful cook, and you've got a
    great set of dishes."

Robin Williams
The Fisher King (1995)

'A husband has certain rights, and a wife has
    certain duties. It's not as much of a chore as
    you may have heard. But if it does become
    one, the best thing to do is just think about
    cannin' apricots."

Unidentified
Goin' South (1978)

'Revenge is the dish which people of taste
    prefer to eat cold."

Dennis Price
Kind Hearts And Coronets (1949)

'Your grapes are so sour I can smell 'em from
    here."

Unidentified
Cover Girl (1944)

EIGHTEEN

HAPPINESS

"You have the most bizarre sense of humor."
"Bizarre people often do."

Maggie Smith and Michael Caine
California Suite (1989)

"Haven't you ever met a man who could make
    you happy?"
"Sure, lots of times."

Cary Grant and Mae West
She Done Him Wrong (1933)

"So, what do you want to talk about?"
"Oh, life."
"It's a bowl of cherries, haven't you heard?
    Want to talk about your cherries or mine?"

Edward Herrmann and Tim Matheson
A Little Sex (1982)

"Happiness is plaguing me."

Salvo Randone
Fellini Satyricon (1969)

"Oh, you do have a sense of humor. I was
   beginning to think you had it surgically
   removed."

Nick Nolte
The Prince Of Tides (1991)

"I haven't got love. I haven't got happiness.
   I've got a 360-degree bed, and 180-degrees
   of it are empty."

Walter Matthau
Plaza Suite (1971)

NINETEEN

HOMOSEXUALITY

"Straight! He's about as straight as the Yellow Brick Road."

Laurence Luckinbill
The Boys In The Band (1970)

"You're kidding. You really are queer? But you're so attractive."

Leslie Ann Warren
Victor/Victoria (1983)

"I don't think you understand, I'm not into boys."
"I'm not either. I'm into men."

Mark Costello and unidentified
Hollywood Hot Tubs (1984)

"You're not gay? What are you—a social worker or something?"

Unidentified
The Ritz (1976)

"Not every woman is a lesbian."
"I'm aware of that unfortunate fact."
Susannah York and Beryl Reid
The Killing Of Sister George (1969)

"It's not as if I'm gay. I'm just curious."
Michael Ontkean
Making Love (1982)

"Why do you think I'm a homosexual?"
"I guess it's because you never talk about
     girls."
"I never talk about dogs either. Does that
     make me a cocker spaniel?"
Corey Parker and Matthew Broderick
Biloxi Blues (1988)

"It's just a phase you're going through. Last
     year it was miniature golf."
Kay Ballard
The Ritz (1976)

"You and Ned are really becoming a Batman
     and Robin."
Meg Foster
A Different Story (1979)

"For years my dad's been telling me teenage
    boys want just one thing. I always thought
    he meant girls."

Michelle Meyrink
The Joy Of Sex (1984)

"He does look a little soft."
"Soft! He looks like Liberace."

William Petersen and Bob Hoskins
Passed Away (1992)

"Sometimes I wish I could boldly go where no
    man has gone before."

Dana Carvey
Wayne's World (1992)

"I'll never ever get into Harvard now. I'll have
    to settle for Queens College."
"Well, you should feel right at home."

Malcolm Dundas and Kevin Dillon
Heaven Help Us (1985)

"Alternative lifestyle, my ass!"

Frederick Forrest
Falling Down (1993)

"If the world was run right, only women
    would get married."
"Hey, can they do that?"

> *Bing Crosby and Bob Hope*
> *Road To Singapore* (1940)

"Listen, I wasn't thrilled about it either,
    thinking I was one of them. But you know it
    is the only fraternity I ever rushed that let
    me in."

> *John Glover*
> *An Early Frost* (1985)

"The last time I went back they passed a bill
    making homosexuality legal. I said to my
    wife, 'Let's get out of here before they make
    it compulsory.'"

> *James Villiers*
> *Saint Jack* (1979)

"This ain't no garden party."
"Well, I may not know my gardens but I know
    a pansy when I see one."

> *Michael Greer and prison guard*
> *Fortune And Men's Eyes* (1971)

"Do you think a homosexual elephant has a
    terrible time of it?"

John Hurt
The Naked Civil Servant (1980)

"Another twenty-five years and you'll be able
    to shake their hands in broad daylight."

Gene Wilder
Blazing Saddles (1974)

"You know, you're a gay man trapped in a
    woman's body."

Craig Chester
Grief (1993)

"I have been called 'Negro' and 'queer,' but I've
    never been called 'French.'"

Benny Luke
La Cage Aux Folles (1979)

"Believe it or not, there was a time in my life
    when I didn't go around announcing I was
    a faggot."
"Well, that must have been before speech
    replaced sign language."

Kenneth Nelson and Frederick Combs
The Boys In The Band (1970)

"Who wants to be felt up by faggots?"
"I can think of two people in this room who
     would love it."
                    Gerry Salzberg and Craig Russell
                              Outrageous! (1977)

"Would you please get out of my face you sorry
     lookin' faggot."
"Who you callin' sorry-lookin'?"
                    Bill Duke and Antonio Fargas
                              Car Wash (1976)

"If I was a butt cowboy I wouldn't even throw
     you to the posse."
"No you wouldn't, you'd keep me for
     yourself."
                    Michael Madsen and Chris Penn
                              Reservoir Dogs (1992)

"We fit together."
"All men and women fit together. Well, even
     some men fit together."
                    Julie Delpy and Eric Stoltz
                              Killing Zoe (1994)

"I think he likes you."
"Yeah, he's nice, but you know, he's a man."
                              Julie Brown and Kathy Griffin
                              Shakes The Clown (1992)

"Maybe I'd have better luck with women."
"I don't know Candy, I can't see you as
    a dyke."
"Please! I'd be a lesbian."
                              Ruth Marshall and Thomas Gibson
                              Love And Human Remains (1995)

"Do you ever get tired of being a professional
    faggot?"
                              Ruth Marshall
                              Love And Human Remains (1995)

"You know the difference between straight
    guys and gay guys?"
"I forget."
"There isn't any. Straight guys are jerks. Gay
    guys are jerks."
                              Steve Buscemi and Richard Ganoung
                              Parting Glances (1986)

"What were you thinking about while we were
    doing it?"
"Willie Mays."

Diane Keaton and Woody Allen
Play It Again, Sam (1972)

"I think heterosexuality is going to make a
    comeback."
"Not if you have anything to do with it!"

James Remar and Whoopi Goldberg
Boys On The Side (1995)

"Are either of you homosexuals?"
"You mean, like flaming?"
"Naw, we're not homosexuals, but we are
    willing to learn."

Bill Lucking, Harold Ramis and Bill Murray
Stripes (1981)

"You lack the imagination to be a homosexual."

Unidentified
Improper Conduct (1984)

"My prospects were bleaker than a gerbil's in a
    bathhouse."

Leslie Nielsen
Naked Gun 33-1/3: The Final Insult (1993)

TWENTY

KISSING

"You wanna dance or would you rather just
suck face?"

Henry Fonda
On Golden Pond (1981)

"I'd love to kiss you but I just washed my hair."
Bette Davis
Cabin In The Cotton (1932)

"I don't like you anymore and I certainly don't
love you. Do we have to have sex?"
"Oh, yes."
"Okay, but no kissing."
Kim Basinger and John Larroquette
Blind Date (1987)

"By night's end I predict that me and her will
interface."

Unidentified
Sixteen Candles (1984)

Kiss me, Larry."
Oh no, I can't, I musn't, I don't even know
    you and besides, I've given up kissing
    strange women."
What made you stop?"
Strange women."

Madeleine Carroll and Bob Hope
My Favorite Blonde (1942)

He sure didn't kiss like it was the first time."
Well, Bo picks up things real fast."

Marilyn Monroe and Arthur O'Connell
Bus Stop (1956)

You know, for a lawyer, you're some good
    kisser."

Jane Fonda
Barefoot In The Park (1967)

I think I'm going to kiss you."
When will you know for sure?"

Walter Matthau and Ingrid Bergman
Cactus Flower (1969)

TWENTY-ONE

LAW

"You're a lawyer aren't you?"
"I practice before the bar—also behind it."
Marilyn Monroe and Jack Paa
Love Nest (1951

"What's more stupid than a policeman? Two policemen."

Unidentifie
Cross My Heart (1992

"That cop couldn't find his dick with two hands and a map."

Ed Harri
Glengarry Glen Ross (1992

"Exactly what are you rebelling against?"
"Well, that depends—whatcha got? "
Steven Antin and Stephen Dor
S.F.W. (1994

"I don't know anything about you that's not
 police business."
"You know I don't wear any underwear, don't
 you Nick?"
Michael Douglas and Sharon Stone
Basic Instinct (1992)

"You know, it's legal for me to take you down
 to the station and sweat it out of you under
 the lights."
"I sweat a lot better in the dark."
Warren Beatty and Madonna
Dick Tracy (1990)

"Now how could you think I was Lt. Branigan?
 We don't even use the same perfume."
Vivian Blaine
Guys And Dolls (1955)

"You got a lawyer?"
"Why, do I need one?"
"This is America, everyone needs a lawyer."
Mathew McCurley and ElijahWood
North (1994)

"You're shaking the law by the tail, and I don't
    like it."

Spencer Tracy
Adam's Rib (1949)

"Is that how you feel about it?"
"I'm a policeman, sir. I don't have feelings."
Dirk Bogarde and John Barrie
Victim (1961)

"Why do you want to be a cop?"
"I like to dress like a man."
"So do I."

Steve Guttenberg and Kim Cattrall
Police Academy (1984)

"Experience has taught me that people just
    don't up and fuck themselves. They need
    somebody else to fuck them, and that's why
    God created lawyers."

Pamela Giddy
S.F.W. (1994)

"Nothing smells as bad as a rotten cop."
Unidentified
Cleopatra Jones (1973)

"I don't like lawyers, they consort with
   criminals."
"No they don't, they consort with other
   lawyers."
"That's what I said."
Miranda Richardson and Adrian Dunbar
Widows' Peak (1994)

"You are a criminal mastermind."
"It's just a hobby."
Bill Pullman and Linda Fiorentino
The Last Seduction (1993)

"What are you, a fucking lawyer?"
"Depends on who I'm with."
Danny DeVito and Penelope Ann Miller
Other People's Money (1991)

"You still a lawyer Frank?"
"Yeah, you still a self-serving bitch?"
Linda Fiorentino and J.T. Walsh
The Last Seduction (1993)

"People usually get what they deserve—except
   for lawyers."
Joe Mantegna
Body Of Evidence (1993)

TWENTY-TWO

LIARS

"You're a thief…and a liar…completely
  untrustworthy."
"A thief and a liar yes, but not untrustworthy."
Rock Hudson and Walter Slezak
Come September (1961)

"There's a perfectly good explanation for this,
  which I'll make up later."

Bug Hall
The Little Rascals (1994)

"I lied about everything—you've got to believe
  me."

John Candy
Once Upon A Crime (1992)

"If I didn't know you, I'd think you were
  telling the truth."

George Peppard
The Strange One (1952)

"You're lying."
"Of course I am, but hear me out."
John Savident and John Turturro
Brain Donors (1992)

"The only people who make love all the time
     are liars."
Louis Jordan
Gigi (1958)

'As Dad always said, a man who can't be
     bribed can't be trusted."
Tony Randall
Lover Come Back (1961)

"The trouble is you stink at lying."
"Excuse me, 'O Queen of Crap."
Steve Martin and Goldie Hawn
Housesitter (1992)

"What you see before you is a masterpiece of
     deception."
Kenneth Nelson
The Boys In The Band (1970)

"When it comes to sex, men can't help from
    lying and women can't keep from telling the
    truth."

Kim Novak
Boys' Night Out (1962)

"Can I speak frankly?"
"Anything's possible."
Alexander Godunov and Shelley Long
The Money Pit (1986)

"Son, this is a Washington, D.C., kind of lie. It's
    when the other person knows you're lying
    and also knows you know he knows."

Henry Fonda
Advise And Consent (1962)

"You're the Ernest Hemingway of bullshit!"
Steve Martin
Housesitter (1992)

TWENTY-THREE

LOVE

"I never had sex with someone that I loved before."

Ethan Hawke
Reality Bites (1994)

"True love is like the Loch Ness monster—everyone has heard of it but no one's ever seen it."

Meshach Taylor
Mannequin Two: On The Move (1991)

"Were you ever in love?"
"Oh, no sir, but I've been married."

Hugh Herbert and Eric Blore
To Beat The Band (1935)

"Why be miserable with someone you don't love? It's better to be miserable with someone you do love."

Gina Lollobrigida
Come September (1961)

"For me love has to go very deep. Sex only has
    to go a few inches."

Unidentified
Bullets Over Broadway (1994)

"A fish and a bird can fall in love, but where
    will they build their nest?"

Erica Yohn
Corrina, Corrina (1994)

"Do you believe in love at first sight?"
"Well, it saves a lot of time."

George Raft and Ann Sheridan
They Drive By Night (1940)

"The next time you have the need to say 'I love
    you' to someone, say it to yourself—
    and see if *you* believe it."

Harvey Fierstein
Torch Song Trilogy (1988)

"Which do you prefer, young boys or mature
    men?"
"I think that when you really love somebody,
    age shouldn't matter at all!"

Mike Kopscha and Kevin Coughlin
The Gay Deceivers (1969)

"My husband and I fell in love at first sight.
Maybe I should have taken a second look."
Mia Farrow
Crimes And Misdemeanors (1989)

"I didn't want to marry anyone, much less
someone who loved me."
Sarah Trigger
Don't Do It! (1995)

"I've never felt that true love should stand in
the way of a good time."
Anne Bancroft
To Be Or Not To Be (1984)

"I cannot believe that a No. 1 business man like
you could let himself go and fall in love
with his own fiancée."
Johnny Silver
Guys And Dolls (1955)

"Have you ever been in love?"
"Yes, for as long as I can remember—with
myself."
Laurence Harvey and Julie Christie
Darling (1965)

"Love is an intoxication."
"And marriage is the hangover."

Unidentified and Bert Wheeler
Cracked Nuts (1931)

"I'm not asking for love."
"Wise man."

Peter Berg and Linda Fiorentino
The Last Seduction (1993)

"A wise woman patterns her life on the
theories and practices of modern banking.
She never gives her love, but only lends it
on the best security and the highest rate of
interest."

Jose Ferrer
Moulin Rouge (1952)

"I knew I was in love. First of all, I was very
nauseous."

Woody Allen
Take The Money And Run (1969)

MARRIAGE

"Aren't you forgetting that you're married?"
"I'm doing my best."

> *Unidentified and Mae West*
> *My Little Chickadee* (1939)

"Marriage is punishment for shoplifting in
 some countries."

> *Mike Myers*
> *Wayne's World* (1992)

"A wedding is a funeral where you smell your
 own flowers."

> *Eddie Cantor*
> *Kid Millions* (1934)

"If you're going to invest two dollars in a
 marriage license, you should get your
 money's worth."

> *Betsy Drake*
> *Will Success Spoil Rock Hunter?* (1957)

"At the rate we're having sex we may as well
    be married already."

Geena Davis
Earth Girls Are Easy (1989)

"'Shut up?' You can't talk to me like that until
    after we're married."

Bob Hope
Son Of Paleface (1952)

"It's no crime being married. It's just a
    weakness that men have that women take
    advantage of."

Fred Astaire
The Gay Divorcee (1931)

"No more Mr. Nice Guy, I want an answer and
    I want it now."
"Is that a threat?"
"No, it's a proposal."

Tim Matheson and Kate Capshaw
A Little Sex (1982)

"I never trust men that are too charming—
    that's why I married you."

June Haver
Love Nest (1951)

"You're not gonna break up a poker game are
     ya?"
"Me, never. Marriage may come and go, but the
     game must go on."
                            Walter Matthau and Jack Lemmon
                                     The Odd Couple (1968)

"What are you doing?"
"I'm adding romance to our lives."
"But we're married."
                            Michael Manteil and Annabella Sciorra
                                   The Night We Never Met (1993)

"I never mix business with pleasure."
"I'm not talking about pleasure, I'm talking
     about you marrying my dad."
                            Melanie Griffith and Michael Patrick Carter
                                              Milk Money (1994)

"I can hardly wait until we're married."
"Why?"
"Because then I'll never have to have sex with
     you again."
                                    Meg Tilly and Eric Stoltz
                                      Sleep With Me (1994)

"How old are you?"
"Twenty-four."
"Are you married?"
"Sometimes."

Brad Renfro and Amy Hathaway
The Client (1994)

"Marriage is like an institution."
"So is Alcatraz, but I wouldn't want to live
    in it."

Lucille Ball and Charlie McCarthy
Look Who's Laughing (1941)

"No matter who you marry, you wake up
    married to someone else."

Marlon Brando
Guys And Dolls (1955)

"It's hard to believe that you haven't had sex
    in 200 years."
"Two hundred and four if you count my
    marriage."

Diane Keaton and Woody Allen
Sleeper (1973)

"Are you sexually active?"
"I'd say I'm experiencing a dry spell."
"So, you're married?"

> *Lisa Banes and Sarah Jessica Parker*
> *Miami Rhapsody* (1995)

"I don't believe in matrimony, it screws up a
    relationship."

> *Burt Reynolds*
> *The Best Little Whorehouse In Texas* (1982)

"I don't know much about women—I've been
    married for twenty-eight years."

> *Wallace Beery*
> *Grand Hotel* (1932)

"Have you ever been married?"
"Once, but I got rid of her. Now I just lease."

> *Jack Lemmon and Walter Matthau*
> *Buddy Buddy* (1981)

"I don't suppose you believe in marriage,
    do you?"
"Only as a last resort."

> *William B. Davidson and Mae West*
> *I'm No Angel* (1933)

"You're not having sex with him, are you?"
"You know that once I move in with a man I
    stop having sex with him."

Rob Schneider and Lea Thompson
The Beverly Hillbillies (1993)

"You married?"
"Occasionally. I'm always on the lookout for a
    future ex-Mrs. Malcolm.

Sam Neill and Jeff Goldblum
Jurassic Park (1993)

"I'm a married woman."
"Meaning what?"
"Meaning I'm not looking for company."
"Then you should have said happily married."

Kathleen Turner and William Hurt
Body Heat (1981)

"Marriage is when a woman asks a man to
    remove his pajamas because she wants to
    send them to the laundry."

Albert Finney
Two For The Road (1967)

"I'll have you know I was asked a thousand
    times to get married."
"Who asked you?"
"My father."

> *Unidentified and Eddie Cantor*
> *Kid Millions* (1934)

"I can't marry her, she's my friend!"

> *Jonathan Taylor Thomas*
> *The Lion King* (1994)

"You will pay dearly for what you have done.
    You will marry me."

> *Ron Perlman*
> *Police Academy: Mission To Moscow* (1994)

Pardon me, but your husband is showing."

> *Glenn Ford*
> *Gilda* (1946)

Men marry because they are tired, women
    marry because they are curious, and both
    are disappointed."

> *George Sanders*
> *The Picture Of Dorian Gray* (1945)

"You lookin' for a friend Trixie?"
"I don't need a friend, I got a husband."
Darnell Williams and Jennifer Jason Leigh
Short Cuts (1993)

"I want you to unlock that door, come out of
    that bathroom and get married."
Lee Grant
Plaza Suite (1971)

"Didn't you always think that women were
    dying to get married?"
"Not to me."
Judd Nelson and Jon Cutler
St. Elmo's Fire (1985)

"I've been married three times."
"You're kidding."
"No, that's the good thing about marriage. It's
    the only real cure for divorce."
Wallace Shawn
A Little Sex (1982)

"Why would a guy want to marry a guy?"
"Security."
Tony Curtis and Jack Lemmon
Some Like It Hot (1959)

"Forgive me for mistrusting you ... it's just that you have been a little distant these last twenty-nine years."

Unidentified
A Funny Thing Happened
On The Way To The Forum (1966)

"Are you aware that your husband is responsible for making thousands of people miserable?"
"Really? And I thought he was just irritating me."

Lauren Hutton and Brenda Vaccaro
Zorro, The Gay Blade (1981)

"You really can't get a divorce?"
"Never. You can't get a divorce without collusion, and she won't collude."

Veronica Lake and Joel McCrea
Sullivan's Travels (1941)

"Your divorce is better than some people's marriage."

Paul Reiser
Bye Bye Love (1995)

"To be in love with a woman who scorns you is
    a problem; to be in love with a man who
    scorns you is a dilemma; but to be in love
    with your ex-wife is a tragedy."

George Sega
Blume In Love (1973

"Are you still on speaking terms with your last
    husband?"
"Oh, sure, I never let a divorce break up a
    friendship."

Linda Darnell and Binnie Barnes
Day Time Wife (1949

"It's so refreshing to hear a man speak so
    highly of the woman he's divorcing."

Monica Evans
The Odd Couple (1968

"Look at the facts."
"I know, I know, fifty-percent of all marriages
    end in divorce."
"Not to mention the ones that end in gunplay."

Gil Bellows and Sarah Jessica Parke
Miami Rhapsody (1995

"I'm getting married on June nineteenth, and I
    want you girls to be there."
"We've never missed one of your weddings."
                    Lainie Kazan and Diane Ladd
                    The Cemetery Club (1993)

"You're like the Ross Perot of matrimony."
                    Sarah Jessica Parker
                    Miami Rhapsody (1995)

"I want you three to be bridesmaids."
"What happened to the ones you used the last
    time?"
"I never use the same bridesmaids twice, it's
    bad luck."
                    Lainie Kazan and Olympia Dukakis
                    The Cemetery Club (1993)

"If you were my husband, I'd give you
    poison."
"If I were your husband, I'd take it."
                    Margaret Hamilton and Billy Gilbert
                    Paradise Alley (1961)

TWENTY-FIVE

MASTURBATION

"Hey, bartender, this guy's playing with
   himself."
"So just ignore him."
"I can't, he's using my hand!"

Unidentified
If You Don't Stop It…You'll Go Blind (1978)

"Don't knock masturbation. It's sex with
   someone I love."

Woody Allen
Annie Hall (1977)

"You wanna play poker with me little lady?"
"Looks like you're having a pretty good time
   playing with yourself."

Lance Henriksen and Sharon Stone
The Quick And The Dead (1994)

"Have a wank? It would be easier to raise the
   Titanic!"

Alfred Molina
Prick Up Your Ears (1987)

"You know, I always suggest that we think of
    the sex drive as we would a fine violin. Play
    it regularly, as it were, and it stays in tune,
    responding to your slightest touch."
Martin Gabel
Divorce, American Style (1967)

"I was naughty all day yesterday."
"Not with me you weren't."
"You'll just have to learn to show up on time."
Michael Caine and Maggie Smith
California Suite (1989)

"Talking to Zuzu was like masturbating with a
    cheese grater—slightly amusing, but mostly
    painful."
Andrew Dice Clay
The Adventures Of Ford Fairlane (1990)

"It's important to have a job that makes a
    difference, boy. That's why I manually
    masturbate caged animals for artificial
    insemination."
Virginia Smith
Clerks (1994)

"Why don't you run outside and jerk yourself a
   soda."

Annette Bening
Bugsy (1991)

"Writing is one-tenth perspiration and nine-
   tenths masturbation."

Gary Oldman
Prick Up Your Ears (1987)

"Time sure flies when you're young and jerking
   off."

Leonardo Di Caprio
The Basketball Diaries (1995)

TWENTY-SIX

MEN

"The only difference between men is the color of their ties."

Helen Broderick
Top Hat (1935)

"I'll be darned, you're a heterosexual."
"And a darned good one!"

Mark Harmon and Robin Thomas
Summer School (1987)

"A few minutes ago I liked Hugo better, now I like you better. It's funny how men change."

Shirley Temple
The Bachelor And The Bobby-Soxer (1947)

"Let's step outside and settle this like men."
"We are outside."
"Then why don't we step inside and settle this like women?"

John Turturro and John Savident
Brain Donors (1992)

"Guys like that, you know, give clowns a bad name."

Bobcat Goldthwait
Shakes The Clown (1992)

"I'm twice the man you are."
"So is she and it's driving me mad."

John Savident and John Turturro
Brain Donors (1992)

"Honey, I'm more man than you'll ever be and more woman than you'll ever get."

Antonio Fargas
Car Wash (1976)

"Which are you, man or boy? It doesn't matter, I'm partial to both."

Kathleen Turner
Naked In New York (1994)

"I think all men are dogs. All men start barking sooner or later."

Octavia Saint Laurent
Paris Is Burning (1991)

"I never liked a man I didn't meet."
Jennifer Jason Leigh
Mrs. Parker And The Vicious Circle (1994)

"I'd kick you in the balls, if you had any."
Ione Skye
Gas Food Lodging (1992)

"I'm only half a man."
"It's the right half."
Norman Kaye and Alyson Best
Man Of Flowers (1984)

"Bulls are bulls, and roosters don't try to lay
    eggs."
Charles Durning
Tootsie (1982)

"Every man I meet wants to protect me. I can't
    figure out what from."
Mae West
My Little Chickadee (1939)

"You've got me so convinced, I may even go
    out and become a woman."
"And you wouldn't have far to go either."
David Wayne and Spencer Tracy
Adam's Rib (1949)

"Tall, dark and tidy, that's a magic
  combination."

Mark Harmon
Summer School (1987)

"I'm fighting my prejudices, but it's clear that
  you're acting—well I hate to put it this
  way—like a man."
"You watch your language."

Katharine Hepburn and David Wayne
Adam's Rib (1949)

"You don't understand, I'm a man."
" Well, nobody's perfect."

Jack Lemmon and Joe E. Brown
Some Like It Hot (1959)

"Pretending to be a man has its disad-
  vantages."

Robert Preston
Victor/Victoria (1983)

"Balls, said the queen. If I had 'em, I'd be king."

Jill Clayburgh
An Unmarried Woman (1978)

"There are no men anymore … facsimiles,
   that's all, facsimiles."

Angela Lansbury
Something For Everyone (1970)

"Men are at their best when women are at their
   worst."

Mae West
Klondike Annie (1936)

"Women today are better hung than the men."
Jack Nicholson
Carnal Knowledge (1970)

"Which of them comes closest?"
"To Casanova?"
"To a man!"

Basil Rathbone and Joan Fontaine
Casanova's Big Night (1954)

"You were in the Marines!"
"Yes, they were looking for a few good men
   and so was I!"

William Ragsdale and Meshach Taylor
Mannequin Two: On The Move (1991)

TWENTY-SEVEN

MILITARY

"I once asked a sailor, 'Would you help a girl in
    trouble?' and he said, 'Depends on the kind
of trouble she wants to get into.'"

Helen O'Connell
The Fleet's In (1942)

"You're like a nuclear menace; your warhead
    should be dismantled."

Sarah Jessica Parker
Miami Rhapsody (1995)

"During this time of the year these slippery
    little creatures come up on the beach, stop,
    spawn and then go out to sea again."
"Sounds like some naval officers I know."

Unidentified and Anne Francis
Don't Go Near The Water (1957)

"They say the Navy makes men. Well, I'm
    liviing proof. They made me."

George Hamilton
Zorro, The Gay Blade (1981)

TWENTY-EIGHT

MONEY

"He's obviously after your money and social
   standing, but I was here first."

John Turturro
Brain Donors (1992)

"You pay your way through life as if every
   relationship were a toll booth."

Sylvia Sidney
Summer Wishes, Winter Dreams (1973)

"I was once so poor I didn't know where my
   next husband was coming from."

Mae West
She Done Him Wrong (1933)

"I don't need money. What I need are questions
   answered. Question one, can I have some
   money?"

Andrew Dice Clay
The Adventures Of Ford Fairlane (1990)

"Do you know what $25,000 buys you today?
    A box of dog biscuits and a disposable
    douche."

> *Anthony Perkins*
> *Deadly Companion* (1986)

"The trouble with you is you're prejudiced
    against me because I'm part of a minority
    group."
"What minority group?"
"Millionaires."

> *Tony Randall and Rock Hudson*
> *Pillow Talk* (1959)

"My idea of taking a risk is shopping at Saks
    without a sale."

> *Rebecca Schaeffer*
> *Scenes From The Class Struggle In Beverly Hills*
> (1989)

"I ask for nothing."
"And you shall receive it in abundance."

> *Patricia Quinn and Tim Curry*
> *The Rocky Horror Picture Show* (1975)

"There are many bonds that will hold us
   together through eternity."
"Really, what are they?"
"Your government bonds, your savings bonds,
   your liberty bonds and maybe a little baby
   bond."

> *Groucho Marx and Margaret Dumont*
> *The Big Store* (1941)

"Of course I loved her! If I didn't love her,
   would I let her put her hands in my cash
   register?"

> *Redd Foxx*
> *Norman ... Is That You?* (1976)

"Don't feel sorry for me. I started out poor and
   worked my way up to outcast."

> *Dolly Parton*
> *The Best Little Whorehouse In Texas* (1982)

"How do you put up with me?"
"Well, you do have seventy-billion dollars."
"Is that the only reason?"
"No, you also have a cute butt."

> *Edward Herrmann and Christine Ebersole*
> *Richie Rich* (1994)

"I've been poor all my life."
"You've got it all wrong honey, you've been
   cheap all your life."

Divine and Lainie Kazan
Lust In The Dust (1985)

"The situation made me take stock of myself
   and evaluate my assets and liabilities."
"I love your assests and liabilities."

Betsy Drake and Tony Randal
Will Success Spoil Rock Hunter? (1957)

"Sex changes everything. I've had relationships
   before where I know a guy and then have
   sex with him, and then I bump into him
   someplace, and he acts like I owe him
   money!"

Teri Garr
Tootsie (1982)

"How could you spend a million dollars in six
   days?"
"You must not have been shopping lately."

Miguel Ferren and Tone Loc
Blank Check (1993)

I told her you spoke two languages. She said
   yes, English and Gucci."
                                    Ron Silver
                              Garbo Talks (1984)

'Do you know what it feels like to be followed
   and hounded and watched every second?"
'Well, I used to. Now I pay cash for
   everything."
                      Madeleine Carroll and Bob Hope
                          My Favorite Blonde (1942)

'The way I see it, you spend $3,000 on a
   bathrobe, you deserve to die."
                                 Robert Beltran
     Scenes From The Class Struggle In Beverly Hills
                                           (1989)

'He who hesitates is poor."
                                    Zero Mostel
                             The Producers (1968)

TWENTY-NINE

MORONS

"It is a moron who gives advice to a horse's
    ass."

> Unidentified
> Victor/Victoria (1983

"Let me leave you with one thought. A mind, a
    good mind, is a terrible thing to waste."
"So is a good body."

> Tony Danza and unidentified
> She's Out Of Control (1989

"He's not exactly plagued by ideas, is he?"

> William Hur
> Mr. Wonderfu

"Don't call me stupid."
"Oh right, to call you stupid would be an insult
    to stupid people."

> Kevin Kline and Jamie Lee Curtis
> A Fish Called Wanda (1989

"What do you think I am, an idiot?"
"No ... I think you're a loser."
Brendan Fraser and Joe Pesci
With Honors (1994)

"You know, man is the only animal clever
   enough to build the Empire State Building
   and stupid enough to jump off it."
Rock Hudson
Come September (1961)

"It seems to me, except for being a little
   mentally ill, she's perfectly normal."
Johnny Depp
Benny & Joon (1993)

"I can't believe you two are from the same gene
   pool."
"He's from the shallow end."
Patricia Wettig and Billy Crystal
City Slickers II: The Legend Of Curly's Gold (1994)

"You're out of your tree."
"It's not my tree."
Mary Stuart Masterson and Johnny Depp
Benny & Joon (1993)

"I don't understand, am I being stupid?"
"No, you're being a man, which is sometimes
     the same thing."

Henry Fonda and Lucille Ball
Yours, Mine And Ours (1968)

"I'll be sober tomorrow, but you'll be crazy the
     rest of your life."

W.C. Fields
It's A Gift (1934)

"I'm only gonna be young once."
"Yeah, but you're gonna be stupid for the rest
     of your life."

Corey Feldman and River Phoenix
Stand By Me (1986)

"I have hemorrhoids smarter than you."

Andrew Divoff
Oblivion (1994)

"This is Professor Einstein, the smartest person
     in the world."
"How they hangin?"

Tony Shalhoub and Frank Whaley
I.Q. (1994)

"Lay off, you know he has a plate in his
 head."
"A plate! I think they threw in the knife and
 fork too!"

Pat Evison and Ross O'Donovan
Starstruck (1982)

"What kind of idiots do you have working
 here?"
"Only the finest in New York City."

Catherine O'Hara and unidentified
Home Alone II: Lost In New York (1992)

"You're a real genius."
"Sorry I can't say the same about you."

Willem Dafoe and Madonna
Body Of Evidence (1993)

"Hate the critics? I have nothing but
 compassion for them. How can I hate the
 crippled, the mentally deficient and the
 dead?"

Albert Finney
The Dresser (1983)

"It's not that I object to your being a bastard.
Don't get me wrong there. It's your being
such a *stupid* bastard that I object to."

Lee Tracy
The Best Man (1964)

"We don't get that sort of thing around here
very often, but we're always on the lookout,
driving around looking for perverts."

Jody Wilson
Radio Inside (1994)

"Don't you want to be smart?"
"No, I want to be like you."

W.C. Fields and Gloria Jean
Never Give A Sucker An Even Break (1941)

"You're not too smart are you? I like that in a
man."
"What else do you like? Lazy, ugly, horney—I
got 'em all."
"You don't look lazy."

Kathleen Turner and William Hurt
Body Heat (1981)

"No questions please, I'm being followed by
    two men in black."
"You sure you don't mean two men in white?"
                    Madeleine Carroll and Bob Hope
                    My Favorite Blonde (1942)

"You seem very intelligent for an American."
"Well, I'm not!"
                    Mira Sorvino and Chris Eigeman
                    Barcelona (1994)

"Can we go? I feel a colossal headache coming
    on."
"I feel one just about to leave."
                    Simon Jones and Robin Williams
                    Club Paradise (1986)

"Why do you always assume the worst about
    people?"
"Statistics."
                    Gil Bellows and Sarah Jessica Parker
                    Miami Rhapsody (1995)

"I hate authors, don't you? ... I wouldn't mind
    them so much if they didn't write books."
                    Polly Walker
                    Enchanted April (1992)

"I wanna be just like you ... all I need is a
   lobotomy and some tights."

Judd Nelson
The Breakfast Club (1985)

"Insanity runs in my family. It practically
   gallops."

Cary Grant
Arsenic And Old Lace (1944)

"I suppose stupid people are too stupid to
   know they're stupid."

Jeanne Moreau
The Summer House (1994)

"I like mental stimulation."
"You tried shock therapy?"

Alan Alda and Mia Farrow
Crimes And Misdemeanors (1989)

"In my case, self-absorption is completely
   justified."

Clifton Webb
Laura (1944)

THIRTY

PLACES

"You're not the only person who's slept with
    thousands of men."
"In Lincoln, Nebraska?'
                    Larry Maraviglia and Slade Burrus
                    The Boys Of Cellblock Q (1993)

"I just love finding new places to wear
    diamonds."
                                Marilyn Monroe
                Gentlemen Prefer Blondes (1953)

"A greater hive of scum and villainy you will
    not find elsewhere in the galaxy."
                                Alec Guinness
                                Star Wars (1977)

"I'm comparatively normal for a man who
    grew up in Brooklyn."
                                Woody Allen
                                Annie Hall (1977)

"What's it feel like to be dead for two-hundred
    years?"
"Like spending a weekend in Beverly Hills."
                    Diane Keaton and Woody Allen
                                Sleeper (1973)

"I want to take you somewhere special."
"In Queens?"
            Marcello Mastroianni and Shirley MacLaine
                                Used People (1992)

"If we destroy Kansas, the world may not hear
    about it for years."

                                    Charles Gray
                        Diamonds Are Forever (1971)

"This is a taxi, madame, not a bedroom!"
                                Ranjit Chowdhry
                        The Night We Never Met (1993)

"They say that all native Californians come
    from Ireland."

                                Fred MacMurray
                        Double Indemnity (1944)

"I must say, you're an island of reality in an
ocean of diarrhea."

Wayne Newton
The Adventures Of Ford Fairlane (1990)

"I don't like the countr; the crickets make me
nervous."

Marlon Brando
On The Waterfront (1954)

"You wanna lighten up on the accent...."
"Look man, I'm from Brooklyn. You're lucky I
can speak English."

Michael J. Fox and Christina Vidal
Life With Mikey (1994)

"I've been things and seen places."

Mae West
She Done Him Wrong (1933)

"What's wrong with Chicago?"
"Nothing a trip to Europe wouldn't cure."

Beah Richards and Anthony Perkins
Mahogany (1975)

"Only in Times Square the dawn gets turned on
    by an electrician."

Marlon Brando
Guys And Dolls (1955)

"Why did you two ever get married?"
"Ah, I don't know. It was raining and we were
    in Pittsburgh."

Helen Broderick
The Bride Walks Out (1936)

"You from Brooklyn?"
"Yonkers."
"What are those?"

Cary Grant and unidentified
I Was A Male War Bride (1940)

"What state were you born in?"
"Infancy."

Brendan Fraser and Joe Pesci
With Honors (1994)

"This is a movie? "
"No, this is California."

Brian Austin and Arnold Schwarzenegger
The Last Action Hero (1993)

I don't fucking live in the world, I fucking live
     in New York City, so go fuck yourself."
                              Michael Keaton
                              The Paper (1994)

What do they know in Pittsburgh?"
They know what they like."
If they knew what they liked they wouldn't
     live in Pittsburgh."
                    Joel McCrea and Robert Warwick
                         Sullivan's Travels (1941)

I love New York. It's like thousands of straight
     lines just looking for a punchline."
                                 Alan Alda
                    Crimes And Misdemeanors (1989)

Why does my hair only look good in Ohio?"
Everybody's hair does. It's the main reason
     people live there."
               Jonathan Silverman and Jason Bateman
                         Breaking The Rules (1992)

Brooklyn, James."

                              Noel Wheaton
                              Cover Girl (1944)

THIRTY-ONE

POLITICS

"We French are so Democratic, we treat
everyone like shit."

Mario Van Peeble
Identity Crisis (1990

"We haven't had sex since the Bush
administration."
"It's hard to perform in that way when the
Democrats are in power."

Christina Pickles and Joseph Bologn
Revenge Of The Nerds: Nerds In Love (1994

"Who has time for politics when you can get a
facial?"

Kraig Swart
World And Time Enough (1994

"Sex is a little bit like politics—the incumbent
always has the advantage."

Matthew Broderic
The Night We Never Met (1993

THIRTY-TWO

PROMISCUITY

"Aren't you appalled at the promiscuity you
find everywhere?"
"I haven't found it anywhere."
Unidentified and Alan Arkin
Last Of The Red Hot Lovers (1972)

"Can you point out the nymphomaniacs to
me?"
"They'll make themselves known."
Tom Conti and unidentified
Reuben, Reuben (1984)

"I need tending, I need someone to take care of
me, someone to rub my tired muscles,
smooth out the sheets."
"Get married."
"I just need it for tonight."
William Hurt and Kathleen Turner
Body Heat (1981)

"She's been plucked more times than the Rose
    of Tralee."

Unidentified
Caddyshack (1980)

"I started at Amherst and I worked my way
    through the alphabet to Yale. I'm stuck
    there."

Elizabeth Taylor
Butterfield 8 (1960)

"Housework is like bad sex. Everytime I do it I
    swear I'll never do it again, until
    company comes by."

Unidentified
Can't Stop The Music (1980)

"When women go wrong, men go right after
    them."

Mae West
She Done Him Wrong (1933)

"After 347 years of one-night stands, I think I'm
    finally falling in love."

Kevin M. Glover
Love Bites (1988)

'I have never done anything that I was
    ashamed of, Ursula."
'Neither have I."
'Yeah, but nobody ever asked you to."
                        Almira Sessions and Esther Howard
                        Sullivan's Travels (1941)

'Your idea of fidelity is not having more than
    one man in the bed at the same time."
                        Dirk Bogarde
                        Darling (1965)

'I see a man in your future."
'What, only one?"
                        Unidentified and Mae West
                        I'm No Angel (1933)

'I been under the impression that you is a
    one man woman."
'I am. One man at a time."
                        Libby Taylor and Mae West
                        I'm No Angel (1933)

'I'm a one-woman man, and I've had mine,
    thank God."
                        Alan Bates
                        Butley (1973)

"I think it's true the height of the sexual
    revolution is over. I don't go to bed with
    just anyone anymore—I have to be attracted
    to them sexually."

Mira Sorvino
Barcelona (1994)

"Just remember that every relationship starts
    with a one-night stand."

Anthony Edwards
The Sure Thing (1985)

"Whoever you are, I've always depended on
    the kindness of strangers."

Vivien Leigh
A Streetcar Named Desire (1951)

THIRTY-THREE

PROPOSITIONS

"I can be sleazy, just give me a chance."
> David Tom
> *Swing Kids* (1993)

"If meaningless sex is what you want, why
can't you have it with me?"
> Geena Davis
> *Earth Girls Are Easy* (1989)

"Look at me darling. Can't you see what my
eyes are saying?"
"Yes, and you ought to watch your language!"
> Unidentified and Jack Benny
> *The Horn Blows At Midnight* (1945)

"How about coming up to my place for a spot
of heavy breathing."
> Walter Matthau
> *Pete 'N Tillie* (1972)

"Any time you got nothing to do—and lots of
   time to do it—come on up."

Mae West
She Done Him Wrong (1933)

"Do you mind if I get personal?"
"I don't mind if you get familiar."

Cary Grant and Mae West
I'm No Angel (1933)

"Too many girls follow the line of least
   resistance."
"Yeah, but a good line is hard to resist."

Unidentified and Mae West
Klondike Annie (1936)

"If I made a pass at you now what would your
   reaction be?"
"You want the result before you place the bet!"

Peter Sellers and Goldie Hawn
There's A Girl In My Soup (1970)

"That was uncalled for!"
"I could have sworn I heard you call."

Dorothy Malone and Dean Martin
Artists And Models (1955)

"Do you want this body?"
"Is this a trick question?"
> *Sigourney Weaver and Bill Murray*
> *Ghostbusters* (1984)

"This may come as a shock to you, but there are
some men who don't end every sentence in
a proposition."
> *Doris Day*
> *Pillow Talk* (1959)

"Say honey, you and me could make music
together—and right now I feel like the L.A.
Philharmonic."
> *Bob Hope*
> *My Favorite Blonde* (1942)

"If you play your cards right you could have
my body."
"Wouldn't you rather leave it to science?"
> *Alan Alda and Mia Farrow*
> *Crimes And Misdemeanors* (1989)

"I want to party with you, cowboy."
> *Bill Murray*
> *Stripes* (1981)

THIRTY-FOUR

PROSTITUTION

"The world is full of whores. What it really needs is a good bookkeeper."

Shelley Winters
The Balcony (1963)

"What would you say the meaning of life is?"
"You got fifty bucks and I'll show you the meaning of life."

Andrew McCarthy and Anna Maria Horsford
St. Elmo's Fire (1985)

"I may be a prostitute, but I am not promiscuous."

Barbra Streisand
The Owl And The Pussycat (1970)

"I'm no hooker—I'm a housewife. We do it for free."

Cybill Shepherd
Once Upon A Crime (1992)

"You're different than a lot of prostitutes I've
     been with."
"I'm not a prostitute."
"Oh really. Well great then. Can I have my
     $1,000 francs back?"
                          Eric Stoltz and Julie Delpy
                          Killing Zoe (1994)

"I don't pay for sex."
"Oh no, you think that if you get a little wife or
     a girlfriend that you don't pay? You pay,
     then you can never be sure if you're gonna
     get it."
               Andrew McCarthy and Anna Maria Horsford
                          St. Elmo's Fire (1985)

"Frankly, you're beginning to smell, and that's
     a handicap for a stud in New York."
                          Dustin Hoffman
                          Midnight Cowboy (1969)

"Lulubelle, it's you! I didn't recognize you
     standing up."
                          Groucho Marx
                          Go West (1940)

"It's always a business doing pleasure with
     you."

Dolly Parton
The Best Little Whorehouse In Texas (1982)

"You cheap little whore."
"I hate it when someone calls you cheap, don't
     you?"

C. Thomas Howell and Nancy McKeon
Teresa's Tattoo (1994)

"I get the idea. She was a tramp from a long
     line of tramps."

Fred MacMurray
Double Indemnity (1944)

"Hey, your fly's open."
"Of course. I gotta go to work too."

Diane Keaton and Richard Gere
Looking For Mr. Goodbar (1977)

"It's got a waiting list to get in."
"Yeah, I got the same problem."

Unidentified
Street Smart (1987)

"Have you told him that you're in the rent-a-
    body business?"
"I told him, I told him!"
"When?"
"Tomorrow, that's when I told him."

Unidentified and Shirley MacLaine
Sweet Charity (1969)

"A fine woman."
"One of the finest women that ever walked the
    streets."

Unidentified and Mae West
She Done Him Wrong (1933)

"You're a fine example of capitalism at its most
    efficient. You merely take natural resources,
    add the cost of labor and sell the product for
    a reasonable profit."

George Segal
The Owl And The Pussycat (1970)

"You make one-hundred dollars an hour and
    you have a safety pen holding your boot
    up?"

Richard Gere
Pretty Woman (1990)

THIRTY-FIVE

RELIGION

"On a Hassidic scale of sexiness, how do I rate?"
Melanie Griffith
A Stranger Among Us (1992)

"For Catholics, death is a promotion."
Cliff Gorman
All That Jazz (1979)

"If there's one thing I hate, it's a pushy priest."
Geoffrey Lewis
Lust In The Dust (1985)

"These two little queers went into this bar and this big ole bartender looks at them for a long time and finally he asks, 'Are you two sisters?' and they say, 'Hell no, we're not even Catholic.'"

Elizabeth Taylor
Reflections In A Golden Eye (1967)

"I know this woman in the biblical sense, and
    she ain't no nun."

Harvey Keitel
Sister Act (1992)

"That country's been sodomized by religion."
Saeed Jaffrey
My Beautiful Laundrette (1986)

"We don't need no preacher selling us bunk."
"I'm not selling bunk, friend—I'm giving it
    away."

Unidentified and Steve Martin
Leap Of Faith (1992)

"Your soul may belong to God, but your ass is
    mine."

Unidentified
Short Eyes (1977)

"I don't know how he did it but he heard me."
"He's omniscient."
"Yeah, his mother's probably one too."
Kevin Dillon and Malcolm Dundas
Heaven Help Us (1985)

"I thought I was the miracle of your life."
"I thought I was the miracle of your life."
"I love you both. I'm going to try life without
   any miracles for a while."
   Andrew McCarthy, Judd Nelson and Ally Sheedy
   St. Elmo's Fire (1985)

"Confession may be good for the soul, but it's
   bad for sex."

   Alan Feinstein
   Looking For Mr. Goodbar (1977)

"She's not just a girl. She's the only evidence of
   God I can find on this entire planet—with
   the exception of the mystical force that
   removes one of my socks from the dryer
   everytime I do the laundry."

   Emilio Estevez
   St. Elmo's Fire (1985)

"Give blow jobs instead of sermons. You'd be
   more honest—and useful."

   Frederic Gorny
   Wild Reeds (1994)

'If this turns into a nuns' bar, I'm outta here."
Unidentified
Sister Act (1992)

'I generally avoid temptation, unless I can't
    resist it."
Mae West
My Little Chickadee (1939)

'Please don't misunderstand me, it's just so
    unusual for a successful sinner to be
    unhappy about sin."
'My unhappiness came up very suddenly,
    maybe it will go away again."
'We can keep you unhappy son, give us a
    chance."
Jean Simmons, Marlon Brando and Regis Toomey
Guys And Dolls (1955)

'Get to the sin, please."
'Plagiarism, father."
'Alone, or with someone else?"
Kevin Dillon and Malcolm Dundas
Heaven Help Us (1985)

"I can resist anything but temptation."

Nicholas Grac
Salome's Last Dance (1987

"Catholics don't have a patent on guilt."
"No, they're just the No. 1 manufacturers of it.'

Zeljko Ivanek and Talia Balsan
Mass Appeal (1984

"You're too stupid to even be a good bigot."

Scott Colomb
Porky's (1982

"What's his taste in music?"
"Catholic."

Nigel Terry and Bobbie Coltran
Caravaggio (1986

"I never liked song-and-dance theology."

Zeljko Ivanek
Mass Appeal (1984)

"I think if there is a god he takes a lot of long
    lunches."

Kenneth Branagh
Peter's Friends (1992)

"You should be sainted."
"Nah, then I'd have to wear underwear."
Ally Sheedy and Judd Nelson
St. Elmo's Fire (1985)

"I don't go to church. Kneeling bags my
   nylons."
Jan Sterling
Ace In The Hole (1951)

"I like to go to confession straight after I've
   been to the hairdresser. It makes me feels so
   complete, body and soul."
Jeanne Moreau
The Summer House (1994)

"Agatha might commit a sin, but she'd never
   commit a faux pas!"
Lowell Sherman
Bachelor Apartment (1931)

"God always has another custard pie up his
   sleeve."
Lynn Redgrave
Georgy Girl (1966)

THIRTY-SIX

SEX

"Are you lonely or horney … what's your
  problem?"
"I'm Irish, which often gets confused for
  lonely *and* horney."

> *Geena Davis and Stephen Rea*
> *Angie (1993)*

"You must not be found in my room. If
  necessary, I will scream for help."
"Oh, I don't need any help."

> *Audrey Dalton and Bob Hope*
> *Casanova's Big Night (1954)*

"Premature ejaculation means always having to
  say you're sorry."

> *Unidentified*
> *Buddy Buddy (1981)*

"Normal sex is still a novelty to most
  people."

> *Unidentified*
> *Prick Up Your Ears (1987)*

"There's a limit to the number of times I can
   watch a man try to get his leg around the
   back of his neck."

Jeremy Irons
M. Butterfly (1993)

"It's not normal to experience mature love for
   anything with four legs."
"Wait until you see her."

Gene Wilder and Titos Vandis
Everything You Ever Wanted To Know About
Sex ...But Were Afraid To Ask (1972)

"Did you ever smell mothballs?"
"Sure."
"How'd you get their little legs apart?"

Unidentified
Personal Best (1982)

"Come on, they were just talking about you."
"No, what'd they say?"
"They said you weren't fit to sleep with sheep."
"What'd you say?"
"I said you were."

Rick Moranis and Robin Williams
Club Paradise (1986)

"What are you looking at? You never saw a guy that slept with a fish before?"

Tom Hanks
Splash (1984)

"I won't bite."
"Then you're like all the men in this town—all talk and no teeth."

Unidentified and Judy Davis
The New Age (1994)

"You are positively infertile."
"You mean we've been doing it every night for nothing!"

Unidentified and Amy Yasbeck
Problem Child (1990)

"You do know he's a cyborg, don't you?"
"What does it matter when you're in love? Besides, he told me his battery would last at least another seventy-five years."

Brian Bremer and Morgan Fairchild
Test Tube Teens From The Year 2000 (1993)

"Fasten your seatbelts; it's gonna be a bumpy
    night."

Bette Davis
All About Eve (1950)

"I was incredible last night in bed. I never once
    had to sit up and consult the manual."

Woody Allen
Play It Again, Sam (1972)

'You were fantastic last night in bed."
"Well thanks. How do you feel now?"
'I think the Pepto Bismol helped."

Woody Allen and Diane Keaton
Play It Again, Sam (1972)

"The last time I was inside a woman was when
    I visited the Statue Of Liberty."

Woody Allen
Crimes And Misdemeanors (1989)

"What would you do if I told you I'd been
    celibate for six months?"
"Cross my legs."

John Ritter and Alyson Reed
Skin Deep (1989)

THIRTY-SEVEN

SHOW BUSINESS

"What do you do?"
"I'm an actor."
"Oh, really, what restaurant?"

> *Brook Adams and Marty Watt*
> *Almost You* (1984)

"I'm not really a dog trainer; I'm an actress."

> *Madeline Kahn*
> *Won Ton Ton, The Dog Who Saved Hollywood*
> (1976)

"Miss Caswell is an actress. A graduate of the Copacabana School of Dramatic Arts."

> *George Sanders*
> *All About Eve* (1950)

"Face it, our glamour days are over ... There's a time in a performer's career when he must consider comedy."

> *Ugo Tognazzi*
> *La Cage Aux Folles II* (1981)

"You know what I hate most about being a
    public figure?"
"What?"
"The public."

Rita Rudner and Kenneth Branagh
Peter's Friends (1992)

"The people only see the part I play in public.
    Only a few select friends know my private
    parts."

Brenda Vaccaro
Zorro, *The Gay Blade* (1981)

"Sometimes I sing and dance around my house
    in my underwear. That don't make me
    Madonna."

Joan Cusack
Working Girl (1988)

"Do you want to perform sex?"
"Perform sex? I don't think I'm up to a
    performance, but I'll rehearse with you,
    if you like."

Diane Keaton and Woody Allen
Sleeper (1973)

"How many Zsa Zsa Gabors can there be in a
   room at one time!"

Unidentified
Outrageous! (1977)

"All I did was take her to a movie."
"You were out all night with her."
"Could I help it if it was a double feature?"
Bob Hope and unidentified
Road To Singapore (1940)

"Ed hates anything that keeps him from going
   to the movies every night. I guess I'm what
   you call a Garbo widow."
Louise Closser Hale
Dinner At Eight (1933)

"Tell the director he should have his head
   examined. He shouldn't have shot the
   picture, he should have shot himself."
Kirk Douglas
The Bad And The Beautiful (1952)

"I'm still a plumber but I'm trying to get into
   acting full time."

Dom DeLuise
The Last Married Couple In America (1980)

"You've got to listen to me Michael. There are
    no other women like you, you're a man."
"Yes, I realize that of course, but I'm also an
    actress."
> *Sydney Pollack and Dustin Hoffman*
> *Tootsie* (1982)

"To all of you who helped me when I was a
    nobody I'd like to thank you now, because
    I'm sure I'll forget you when I'm big and in
    Hollywood."
> *Glen Plummer*
> *Frankie & Johnny* (1991)

"How do you tell a good script?"
"Does your character die in the script?"
"No."
"Then it's a good script."
> *Robert Townsend and Brad Sanders*
> *Hollywood Shuffle* (1987)

"He's interested in producing something of
    mine."
"Your first child."
> *Mia Farrow and Woody Allen*
> *Crimes And Misdemeanors* (1989)

"If life is a movie, someday you'll look back at this footage and wish you had had a good hairdresser."

Caroline Azar
No Skin Off My Ass (1991)

"Life doesn't imitate art; it imitates bad television."

Juliette Lewis
Husbands And Wives (1992)

"What an interesting concept it is to eliminate the writer from the artistic process. If we can just get rid of these actors and directors maybe we've got something here."

Tim Robbins
The Player (1992)

"A lot of people's lives get in the way of their TV viewing."

Mark Lamos
Longtime Companion (1989)

"There are three important things in life: sex, movies and my career."

Craig Russell
Outrageous! (1977)

"William Shakespeare once wrote a play in five
    days."
"Well, writing a play in five days is nothing.
    Having it run five days is the trick."
Lucille Ball and Bob Hope
Critic's Choice (1963)

"So, you still an actor?"
"No, I got out of it when I was fifteen. I just
    started to hate the superficiality of the
    whole scene. I'm an agent now."
Mario Todisco and Michael J. Fox
Life With Mikey (1994)

"That's your problem. You don't want to be in
    love, you want to be in love in a movie!"
Rosie O'Donnell
Sleepless In Seattle (1993)

"I went to a psychiatrist."
"I was gonna do that too except in Hollywood
    they're so busy with producers you can't
    even get an appointment."
Jayne Mansfield and Joan Blondell
Will Success Spoil Rock Hunter? (1957)

"That's part of your problem, you know, you
    haven't seen enough movies. All of life's
    riddles are answered in the movies."

Steve Martin
Grand Canyon (1991)

"Out here the streets are paved with
    Goldwyn."

Jennifer Jason Leigh
Mrs. Parker And The Vicious Circle (1994)

"We could be the first husband and wife team
    ever nominated for an Oscar."
"Oh shit, now I'll have to see the movie!"

Peter Gallagher and Jennifer Jason Leigh
Mrs. Parker And The Vicious Circle (1994)

"I don't care for musicals, they hurt my ears."

Veronica Lake
Sullivan's Travels (1941)

"I must have killed more men than Cecil B.
    DeMille."

Gene Wilder
Blazing Saddles (1974)

"Listen babe, there's no one bigger than Wayne
   Newton in this town."

Unidentified
Honey, I Blew Up The Kids (1992)

"If ever a plot needed a twist, this one does."

Joel McCrea
Sullivan's Travels (1941)

"Who's Nat Burton?"
"He's my agent."
"Do you think he'll help?"
"He better. If I get the electric chair he gets ten-
   percent of the current."

Madeleine Carroll and Bob Hope
My Favorite Blonde (1942)

"Life is a Zasu Pitts movie!"

Illeana Douglas
Grief (1993)

"You busy tonight?"
"Some old friends are coming over. We're going
   to show some pornographic movies."
"You need an usher?"

Unidentified and Woody Allen
Bananas (1971)

"I want more than just sex."
"That's why God created television."
Ruth Marshall and Thomas Gibson
Love And Human Remains (1995)

"I can't act in a swimsuit!"
Paul Johansson
Soapdish (1991)

"How do you explain the critical success of
    your last movie?"
"The critics obviously didn't understand it."
Unidentified and Bruce LaBruce
Super 8-1/2 (1993)

"You think wedding vows are going to change
    anything? God, your naivete is astonishing.
    Didn't you see *The Graduate*?"
Chris Eigeman
Barcelona (1994)

"I'm not an actor; I'm a movie star!"
Peter O'Toole
My Favorite Year (1982)

THIRTY-EIGHT

STYLE

It's lavish, but I call it home."

Clifton Webb
Laura (1944)

I like to think of life as a limousine. Though
we are all driving together, we must
remember our places. There's the front seat,
and a back seat, and a window in between."

John Williams
Sabrina (1954)

Who was your decorator, Tiny Tim?"

Jo Ann Harris
The Gay Deceivers (1969)

He's a cultural Robin Hood. He steals from
the witty and gives to the dull."

Walter Matthau
Pete 'N' Tillie (1972)

"Poinsettias are the Bob Goulet of botany."

Robert Mors
Tru (1992

"My taste is impeccable, even when it's bad."

Alan Bate
Nijinsky (1980

"Well, that's the pot calling the kettle beige."

Leonard Fre
The Boys In The Band (1970

"He's like a spider and he expects me to
    decorate his web."

Doris Da
Pillow Talk (1959

"Goodness, what beautiful diamonds."
"Goodness had nothing to do with it."

Mae Wes
Night After Night (1932

"You have a way of making a woman feel like a
    one-way train ticket."

Linda Fiorentin
The Last Seduction (1993

"I really like you Tomas. You are the complete
    opposite of kitsch. In the Kingdom of
    Kitsch, you would be a monster."

Lena Olin
The Unbearable Lightness Of Being (1988)

"Look, you wanna touch me, lick me, spank
    me? Do it! But if this poetry shit continues,
    just shoot me, please."

Lori Petty
Tank Girl (1995)

"Not too much culture please. I'm on my
    holiday."

George De La Pena
Nijinsky (1980)

"Who's your decorator?"
"Some fag. Charged me up the ass, you know?"
Priscilla Presley and Andrew Dice Clay
The Adventures Of Ford Fairlane (1990)

"I loaf, but in a highly decorative and charming
    manner."

Zachary Scott
Mildred Pierce (1945)

THIRTY-NINE

TALLYWACKERS

"Can we call it tallywacker? 'Penis' is so
   personal."

> Unidentified
> Porky's (1982)

"Six foot, six inches of opportunity doesn't
   come along every day you know."

> Thelma Ritter
> Pillow Talk (1959)

"My sex life is in your hands."

> Jackie Mason
> The Jerk (1979)

"What ya got there?"
"What's it look like?"
"A prick, only smaller."

> Unidentified and John Sorvino
> Bloodbrothers (1978)

"She could give a dog a bone."

Mike Myers
Wayne's World 2 (1993)

"I hear you have a taste for little boys."
"No Caesar, big boys."

Peter O'Toole and Malcolm McDowell
Caligula (1979)

"Your penis and my brain will be a marriage
    made in hell."

Dennis Hunt
Flesh Gordon Meets The Cosmic Cheerleaders
(1993)

"Do you think it's easy to run when you're
    holding a banana the size of a canoe?"

Woody Allen
Sleeper (1973)

"I need a rubber."
"We don't have any training rubbers."

Dan Monahan and unidentified
Porky's (1982)

"Do you know what this is?"

"Well, that's a wee wee."

"No, no, my dear…from now on we shall call this a prick."

"Come on, I've seen lots of pricks and that is definitely a wee wee."

Unidentified
If You Don't Stop It…You'll Go Blind (1978)

"Is that a cowlick or are you just glad to see me?"

Reba McIntyre
The Little Rascals (1994)

"I was sixteen before I realized I was a boy."

"What convinced you?"

"Gravity."

David Thornton and Jennifer Jason Leigh
Mrs. Parker And The Vicious Circle (1994)

"Hi cowboy. How tall are you without your horse?"

"Well ma'am, I'm six feet, seven inches."

"Never mind the six feet. Let's talk about the seven inches!"

Mae West and unidentified
Myra Breckenridge (1970)

"So, why did the guy give a name to his
    penis? He didn't want a stranger making all
    of his decisions."

Phil Hartman
National Lampoon's Loaded Weapon 1 (1993)

"Pull in your reel, Mr. Fielding. You're barking
    up the wrong fish."

Jack Lemmon
Some Like It Hot (1959)

"Who are you?"
"I'm your worst nightmare."
"No, waking up without my penis is my worst
    nightmare."

Emilio Estevez and Tim Curry
National Lampoon's Loaded Weapon 1 (1993)

"My brain? It's my second-favorite organ."

Woody Allen
Sleeper (1973)

"Hope you're not frightened."
"I'm not, but fortunately my cock is scared
    stiff."

Raye Hollitt and John Ritter
Skin Deep (1989)

"What was the dirtiest thing ever said on
    television?"
"I don't know."
"Ward, I think you were a little hard on the
    Beaver."

Unidentified
Revenge Of The Nerds (1984)

"I'm talkin dick, dick, dick, dick, dick, dick,
    dick, dick, dick, dick, dick, dick."
"How many dicks is that?"
"A lot."

Quentin Tarantino, Eddie Bunker
and Harvey Keitel
Reservoir Dogs (1992)

"My temperature runs a little high ... I don't
    mind, it's the engine or something."
"Maybe you need a tune-up."
"Don't tell me, you have just the right tool."
Kathleen Turner and William Hurt
Body Heat (1981)

"Dames! They're like poison ivy. You rub up
    against them and everything starts to swell."
Unidentified
Man Called Sarge (1970)

"Holy shit! Your hair has a hard-on."
Bette Midler
The Rose (1979)

"I'm afraid you've caught me with more than
my hands up."
Sean Connery
Diamonds Are Forever (1971)

"Is that a gun in your pocket, or are you just
happy to see me?"
Mae West
She Done Him Wrong (1933)

"Gentlemen, start your boners!"
Adrian Zmed
Bachelor Party (1984)

"There's only one way to handle a woman—be
kind but firm!"
"I was firm, but she was firmer."
Unidentified
Wife, Husband And Friend (1939)

"You know what that car represents?"
"It's an extension of your penis. Actually I
   think you're flattering yourself. You ought
   to be driving a compact."
Gene Hackman and unidentified
Loose Cannons (1990)

"You are such a prick."
"Dear boy, some of my best friends are pricks."
"Some of your best pricks are friends."
John Ritter and Peter Donat
Skin Deep (1989)

"It's not the men in your life that counts—it's
   the life in your men."
Mae West
I'm No Angel (1933)

"Remember, a good man is hard to find and a
   hard man is good—good to find."
Richard Benjamin
How To Beat The High Cost Of Living (1980)

"You may call me the Lion of Cashmere."
"You may call *me* the Boner of East L.A."
Andy Bumatai and Paul Rodriguez
The Whoopee Boys (1986)

"It's so quiet up here, you can hear a mouse get
    a hard-on."
                                    John Belushi
                        Continental Divide (1981)

"Was it hard for you in the Resistance?"
"Very hard, but not as hard as it is now."
                        Peter Sellers and unidentified
                    The Pink Panther Strikes Again (1976)

"You're too much of a cunt to be a prick."
                                    John Ritter
                                Skin Deep (1989)

"I told you, I'm putty in your hands."
"What am I going to do with a handful of putty?"
                        Alan Alda and Mia Farrow
                    Crimes And Misdemeanors (1989)

"I think I'm getting excited."
"Let me know when you're sure."
                        James Caan and Bette Midler
                                For The Boys (1991)

"I'd recognize that penis anywhere."
                                Nancy Parsons
                                Porky's (1982)

TITS & ASS

"I never told this to anyone before, but when I
   was a little child I was breast fed from
   falsies."

Woody Allen
Everything You Ever Wanted To Know About
Sex ... But Were Afraid To Ask (1972)

"Cameron's so tight if you stuck a piece of coal
   up his ass, in two weeks you'd have a
   diamond."

Matthew Broderick
Ferris Bueller's Day Off (1986)

"Roy, you have boobs!"
"They're not mine."

Pam Dawber and John Ritter
Stay Tuned (1992)

"How do you do your tits like that?"
"I usually have someone do them for me."

Unidentified and Craig Russell
Outrageous! (1977)

"You are unsophisticated, ignorant and totally
    lacking in social grace, but I console myself
    in the fact that you have nice buttocks."
                                        Unidentified
                                    King Ralph (1991)

"It's got more plastic than Cher."
                                        Mel Gibson
                                Lethal Weapon 3 (1992)

"My tits! Where are my tits?"
                                        Rex Reed
                            Myra Breckenridge (1970)

"I never heard anyone fart like you."
"You're lucky, not many men can make an
    honest living with their asses."
                    Jean Yanne and Maurice Benichou
                                    A La Mode (1994)

"You still have your hourglass figure, my dear,
    but most of the sand has gone to the
    bottom."
                                        Unidentified
                                The Lemon Drop Kid (1951)

"Why is it only my *ass* that ever gets invited
  places?"

Vicki Frederick
A Chorus Line (1985)

"What if my uniform bursts open and oops, my
  bosoms come flying out."
"You think there are men in this country who
  ain't seen your bosom?"

Madonna and Rosie O'Donnell
A League Of Their Own (1992)

"Why use the front door when I can use the
  back door?"

Jason Adams and Paul Marius
I'll Love You Forever ... Tonight (1993)

"Oh my God, I knew it! We enjoyed it! We're
  homos. We're rump rangers."

Thomas Ballatore
Once Bitten (1985)

"I think I know that tush."

Unidentified
Hollywood Hot Tubs (1984)

"They asked to see you together."
"What are they, Siamese twins?"
"No, but I get the feeling that they're joined
    together from time to time."
Mike Kopscha and Kevin Coughlin
The Gay Deceivers (1969)

"Sounds like an Agatha Christie novel—
Sodomy on the Orient Express."
Corey Parker
Biloxi Blues (1988)

"Don't let your mouth get you into something
    your ass can't handle."
Leonardo Di Caprio
The Basketball Diaries (1995)

"For the next eight weeks I'll be all over your
    butt like white on rice."
"Is that a promise?"
Lynn Whitfield and Pauly Shore
In The Army Now (1994)

"You wouldn't know reality if it was stuck up
    your ass."
Raul Julia
Kiss Of The Spider Woman (1985)

"What's up his ass?"
"A bagel."

Unidentified and Michael Keaton
The Paper (1994)

"This beach is dead—it's all preparation and
   no H."

Rick Moranis
Club Paradise (1986)

"I refuse to go out with a man whose ass is
   smaller than mine."

Elizabeth Perkins
About Last Night ... (1986)

"He's got a great ass."
"Too bad it's on his shoulders."

Sandra Beri and Daryl Hannah
Roxanne (1987)

FORTY-ONE

VIOLENCE

"You're using sex like some people use a fly
  swatter."

Cary Grant
North By Northwest (1959)

"So many assholes, so few bullets."

Andrew Dice Clay
The Adventures Of Ford Fairlane (1990)

"You look like a sensitive, intelligent guy. Don't
  make me shoot you."

Sean Young
Stripes (1981)

"Don't torture yourself. That's my job."

Anjelica Huston
The Addams Family (1991)

"You guys don't want to fuck with me. I just
  got fired from the post office."

Keenen Ivory Wayans
Low Down Dirty Shame (1995)

"You know, if you shoot me you'll lose a lot of
these humanitarian awards."

Chevy Chase
Fletch (1985)

"Don't fuck with me, fellas! This ain't my first
time at the rodeo."

Faye Dunaway
Mommie Dearest (1981)

"Isn't he a lady killer?"
"Acquitted."

Raul Julia
Addams Family Values (1993)

"Grab 'em by the balls—their hearts and minds
will follow."

Paul Freeman
Just Like A Woman (1994)

"I will put my foot so far up your ass that the
water on my knee will quench your
thirst."

Damon Wayans
Major Payne (1995)

FORTY-TWO

VIRGINS

"I'm a virgin. I'm just not very good at it."
Valeria Golino
Hot Shots! (19391)

"I guess I'm a non-practicing Jew."
"Hey, I'm a non-practicing virgin!"
Ben Stiller and Winona Ryder
Reality Bites (1994)

"Would you believe I was a virgin when I got
married?"
"So was I according to my publicist."
Mary Woronov and Jacqueline Bisset
Scenes From The Class Struggle In Beverly Hills
(1989)

"She's harder to get into than a Pearl Jam
concert."
Jack Noseworthy
The Brady Bunch Movie (1995)

"I've learned one thing from this whole situation. When it comes to sex, there are certain things that should be left unknown, and with my luck they probably will be."

Woody Allen
Everything You Ever Wanted To Know About Sex ...But Were Afraid To Ask (1972)

"Years from now when you talk about this— and you will—be kind."

Deborah Kerr
Tea & Sympathy (1956)

"I haven't had anything this pure since the Vienna Boys Choir hit town."

Lauren Hutton
Once Bitten (1985)

"I've had more virgins than you've had crabs."

Ray Sharkey
Scenes From The Class Struggle In Beverly Hills (1989)

"Sex happens to be the one subject I can speak about with absolutely no authority whatsoever."

Justin Ross
A Chorus Line (1985)

"I truly believe that if we can get two women
     on the Supreme Court we can get at least
     one on you."

Janeane Garofalo
Reality Bites (1994)

"I was more familiar with Africa than I was
     with my own body, until I was fifteen."

Beryl Reid
Entertaining Mr. Sloane (1970)

"My observations conclude this man is a picky
     eater, afraid of heights and still a virgin."
"I'm not a picky eater!"

Unidentified and Charlie Schlatter
Police Academy: Mission To Moscow (1994)

"There are worse things than chastity."
"Yes—lunacy and death."

Unidentified
The Night Of The Iguana (1964)

"You're a virgin, aren't you?"
"Technically."

Mickey Rourke and Steve Guttenberg
Diner (1982)

FORTY-THREE

WEIGHT

"It takes fourteen hours of solid exercise to lose a pound of fat."
"How long for a pound of bullshit?"
Ken Higelin and Francois Hautesserre
A La Mode (1994)

"That's no love handle, that's a hate handle."
Alan Rosenberg
Happy Birthday, Gemini (1980)

"You've gained weight."
"Yes, now I'm almost your size. "
Unidentified
Vegas In Space (1993)

"Don't be so free with your hands."
"Listen honey, I was only trying to guess your weight."
Unidentified and W.C. Fields
Never Give A Sucker An Even Break (1941)

"Do these come in my size?"
"You've got to be kidding. Try the Parachute
    pavilion."

Unidentified
Vegas In Space (1993)

"I'm fat, I'm thin, I'm fat, I'm thin …."
"Well, look at it this way, you always wanted to
    look like Elizabeth Taylor and now you do."
Joyce Van Patten and Mare Winningham
St. Elmo's Fire (1985)

"For one dollar I'll guess your weight, your
    height and your sex."

Steve Martin
The Jerk (1979)

FORTY-FOUR

WOMEN

"Women need a reason to have sex; men just need a place."

Billy Crystal
City Slickers (1991)

"Statistics show that there are more women in the world than anything else—except insects."

Rita Hayworth
Gilda (1946)

"It's funny, I haven't thought of women in weeks."
"I fail to see the humor."

Jack Lemmon and Walter Matthau
The Odd Couple (1968)

"You know, there's a saying, a woman without a man is like a fish without a bicycle."

Sandra Dumas
Twice A Woman (1985)

"You smell like you've been with a woman."
"No it's vomit."

Angela Pleasance and Bob Hoskins
The Favor, The Watch And The Very Big Fish
(1992)

"I thought we agreed that women and
    gambling don't mix."
"My wife doesn't come under the category
    of women."

Glenn Ford and George Macready
Gilda (1946)

"Let me tell you something about women.
    They're selfish, they're conniving, and if
    you don't care too much for dancing, you
    don't need them at all."

Redd Foxx
Norman ... Is That You? (1976)

"Tudi's not just a clown, she's a liberated
    woman."

Johanna Went
Grief (1993)

"If there's anything worse than a woman living alone, it's a woman saying she likes it."

Thelma Ritter
Pillow Talk (1959)

"I'm not putting the knock on dolls. It's just that they're something to have around only when they come in handy—like cough drops."

Marlon Brando
Guys And Dolls (1955)

"If you're going to be a degenerate, you might as well be a lady about it."

Olympia Dukakis
Tales Of The City (1993)

"When women go wrong, men go right after them."

Mae West
She Done Him Wrong (1933)

"I've never seen anyone who looked like this before. My mom sure doesn't."
"These aren't moms, these are women!"

Joseph Mazzello and Brad Renfro
The Cure (1995)

FORTY-FIVE

WORK

"This job would be great if it weren't for the
fucking customers."

Jeff Anderson
Clerks (1994)

"This job is turning into work."

Jewell Shephard
Hollywood Hot Tubs (1984)

"You would need three promotions to be an
asshole."

Christopher Walken
Biloxi Blues (1988)

"Before you say or do anything, I want you to
know I'm a minor."
"That's OK, my first wife was a truck driver."

Lori Loughlin and unidentified
The Night Before (1988)

"I can't even read my own writing. I don't do
    shorthand and I can't type."
"How do you keep your job?"
"I give good phone."

> *Jill Clayburgh and Gene Wilder*
> *Silver Streak (1976)*

"Are you a model?"
"No, I'm a cosmetologist."
"Really, a cosmetologist? That's unbelieveable,
    that's impressive. It must be tough to
    handle weightlessness!"

> *Steve Martin and Bernadette Peters*
> *The Jerk (1979)*

"He's the boss. If I could find the right doctor
    I'd have my lips permanently sewed to his
    ass."

> *Peter MacNicol*
> *Housesitter (1992)*

"I had twenty-three jobs last year. How many
    did you have?"
"Just the one."
"Then I'd hardly call you a big job expert."

> *Julia Sweeney and David Foley*
> *It's Pat—The Movie (1994)*

I think next week I'll be able to send more
   money. I may have extra work. My friend
   Patty promised me a blow job."

Steve Martin
The Jerk (1979)

Never burn bridges. Today's junior prick,
   tomorrow's senior partner."

Sigourney Weaver
Working Girl (1988)

I'm really a fairy princess pretending to be a
   waitress."

Heather Graham
Don't Do It! (1995)

He can't get it up. You know, when I married
   a C.P.A. I thought it would be his eyes that
   would go first."

Ellen Burstyn
Same Time Next Year (1978)

I've discovered I have no real talent for
writing, but I can't quit, I'm too famous."

Campbell Scott
Mrs. Parker And The Vicious Circle (1994)

"I've got cancer of the career. It's inoperable."
> *Billy Crysta*
> *Mr. Saturday Night* (1992

"Wow, that looks like a fun job."
"Being a human cannonball is more than a job
    Pee Wee, it's a career."
> *Paul Reubens and Kris Kristoffersoi*
> *Big Top Pee Wee* (1988

"I need something that will amuse a three-year
    old."
"How about my paycheck?"
> *Steve Martin and Catherine O'Har*
> *A Simple Twist Of Fate* (1994

"I don't mix plumbing with pleasure."
> *Donna McDanie.*
> *Hollywood Hot Tubs* (1984)

"That weekend was a mistake."
"Hey, I'm sorry I made you clean the toilets
    and the bathtubs—but who did all the work
    in bed?"
> *Lauren Holly and Andrew Dice Clay*
> *The Adventures Of Ford Fairlane* (1990)

"I don't believe in hell. I believe in un-
    employment, but I don't believe in hell."
                                    Dustin Hoffman
                                    Tootsie (1982)

"Business worries?"
"Nah, business is great. I'm makin' almost
    enough to pay my income tax."
                            Tom Fadden and Bob Hope
                            My Favorite Blonde (1942)

"What exactly does he do, anyway? Is he an
    entreprenuer?"
"No, he's an American."
                        Karen Duffy and Brian Bonsall
                            Blank Check (1993)

"Jack can help us."
"Isn't Jack in jail?"
"No, no, he got off with a small fine. Jack's a
perfectly legitimate real-estate agent."
                        Tom Hanks and Shelley Long
                            The Money Pit (1986)

"As long as they've got sidewalks, you've got a
    job."
                                    Joan Blondell
                            Footlight Parade (1933)

"The point is, you get to capitalize on fellow
   human beings misfortune. That's the basis
   of real estate."

Josh Moste
The Money Pit (1986

"I don't know Walter. I've never been any good
   at that kind of thing."
"What kind of thing?"
"Work."

Shelley Long and Tom Hanks
The Money Pit (1986)

"I should be working in a job that I have some
   kind of aptitude for—like donating sperm
   to an artificial insemination lab."

Woody Allen
Bananas (1971)

"There's not a single job in this town. There's
   nothin, nada, zip."
"Yep, unless you wanna work forty hours a
   week."

Jeff Daniels and Jim Carrey
Dumb & Dumber (1995)

"I thought you were a cynic."
"It's after six—I'm off duty."

Gérard Depardieu and Faith Prince
My Father The Hero (1994)

"Diamonds is my career."

Mae West
She Done Him Wrong (1933)

"How did she come to have sex with a dead
 man?"
"She thought it was me."
"What kind of a convenience store do you run
 here?"

Pattijean Csik and Brian O'Halloran
Clerks (1994)

"Every day, up at the crack of noon."

Lucille Ball
Mame (1974)

"If there's one thing I know, it's men. I ought
 to, it's been my life's work."

Marie Dressler
Dinner At Eight (1933)

AUTHOR

AUTHOR AND FILM BUFF STEVE STEWART HAS written eight books, including the *Gay Hollywood Film & Video Guide*, now in its 2nd edition.

Having spent much of his personal and professional life in Hollywood, he now resides in Orange County, California.

Often asked by interviewers his personal top-10 "campy" films, they are, in alphabetical order: *The Adventures Of Priscilla—Queen Of The Desert*, *The Boys In The Band*, *Calamity Jane*, *Ed Wood*, *Flesh Gordon*, *The Gay Deceivers*, *No Skin Off My Ass*, *The Rocky Horror Picture Show*, *Some Like It Hot*, *The Wizard Of Oz* and, of course, any Busby Berkeley Musical.